BEYOND THE BARS
Ten Walks from York City Walls

with illustrations by the author

by
Ivan E Broadhead

York is the city where all the streets are gates,
all the gates are bars, and all the bars are pubs

. . . an American description

Meridian Books

Published 1989 by Meridian Books.

© Ivan E Broadhead 1989.

British Library Cataloguing in Publication Data.

Broadhead, Ivan E.
  Beyond the Bars: ten walks from York city walls.
  1. North Yorkshire. York - Visitor's guides
  I. Title
  914.28′4304858

  ISBN 1-869922-05-0

Meridian Books
40 Hadzor Road
Oldbury
Warley
West Midlands B68 9LA

Maps by Angela Saunders
Printed in Great Britain by BPCC Wheatons Ltd., Exeter.

Contents

Dedication

To my good friend HAROLD BOOTY, a former librarian,
and to all those other librarians who give so unstintingly
of their knowledge and experience to authors like me.

Acknowledgements

Inspiration and enthusiastic help towards preparing this
book has come from many sources too numerous to detail
here. Much was learned from librarians, teachers, vicars,
boatmen, railwaymen, historians, publicans,
industrialists, authorities, associations, hotel-keepers,
and a variety of individuals who indulged my curiosity,
gave me directions, or whole-heartedly aided me in other
ways.

Encouragement too from many friends and colleagues
gave me the stimulus to persevere, but without the
endless patience and tolerance of my wife, Jean, this book
would never have emerged.

I am particularly indebted to all the library staffs in and
around York, especially York Reference Library, who
offered useful suggestions for detailed research and made
a positive contribution with their willing assistance.

If there are any errors or omissions they are mine, and
mine alone, but every effort has been made to ensure that
the facts are correctly presented.

Maps

Each walk is accompanied by a detailed sketch map. It is, however, often useful to have a more comprehensive map with you in case you want to break your walk or divert to study some other features of the area. A good city map will cover all the walks in this book except for parts of numbers 2 and 9 for which Ordnance Survey Landranger map 105 would be helpful.

Introduction

The addition of yet another book to the considerable number of guides and histories of the city of York might seem altogether unnecessary if there did not appear to be some special reason.

Justification, I believe, can be found in the fact that York is both garlanded and enslaved by its famous medieval walls of magnesian limestone, which afford visitors some fine bird's eye views of the city. The Romans were first to build walls in York to defend their fortress on the site of the Minster. The Vikings later restored and extended them after they had been neglected in the Dark Ages. The Normans extended them even further, creating the line of the walls we know today. Only eighty-four towns in Britain still have any part of their city walls left and York's are the most complete and finest, covering just over two miles in length with four major gates, or Bars, remaining and the site of six lesser gateways or posterns still to be found.

In 1800 York nearly lost its walls altogether. They had become so derelict the City Council applied to Parliament for permission to pull them down. Fortunately permission was refused but not before some demolition had taken place. Public concern resulted in the formation of the York Footpath Society to protect the walls, and one of its members was artist William Etty whose statue clasping a model of Bootham Bar in recognition of his efforts, stands outside the City Art Gallery.

The Victorians restored and opened up the walls as a public promenade and the last stretch of footpath to open was between Bootham and Monk Bar in 1888.

During its 2,000 years as a settlement York has been a city for all seasons and all sorts of people. Above all it may have been visited in the pursuit of history, but also for trade, culture, and popular entertainment; for the discovery of the unexpected that comes from simply wandering around the city. This is a city that can only be savoured on foot and those who wish to appreciate and understand it must be prepared for more than a casual random saunter. Unfortunately the majority of visitors tend to be constrained by the walls and overwhelmed by the cornucopia of attractions within. As a result the treasures outside are largely unknown, unvisited, and generally ignored.

You would be wrong to suppose that the city walls constituted the city's boundaries. They never did at any time in the city's history; never. In time of war they were the defences behind which all the citizens sought refuge; but the boundaries within which the "Mayor and Commonalty of the City of York" exercised jurisdiction extended nearly a mile in all directions beyond the walls.

Hardly a month passes that does not witness the removal of some feature of former days. Even the ancient significant names of some of our eminent streets have not been spared, but have been needlessly abolished with unmeaning and inapplicable substitutes adopted.

I hope you will feel that an attempt to snatch from oblivion some of these bygone things — to recall to your observation some of the few vestiges of suburban antiquity that still remain in our streets and connect them with historical associations before all traces of their original aspect and external forms are wholly swept away — may not be deemed altogether useless or uninteresting. For the suburbs of York are one of its secret delights.

I intend to make this attempt by inviting you to accompany me in some rambles through our suburban streets, lanes, highways, byways and open spaces; and should I occasionally dwell on structures of comparative modernity, or introduce a sprinkling of anecdote suggested by the localities in which we happen to be, it may serve to relieve in some degree the dryness of descriptive detail.

For those people prepared to venture beyond the walls, for those people with a discerning eye, for those people with a little more leisure time to spare, this book sets out to illuminate and point out the right directions. The information it provides is intended to whet the appetites of those who, like the archaeologist, are eager to dig a little deeper into the fascinating story that makes great this city of York. Hopefully you will echo the poet who wrote:

By you transported; we securely stray
Where the winding paths lead the doubtful way;
The silent lane and expansive green to explore
And long perplexing streets untrod before.

Ivan E Broadhead
York 1989

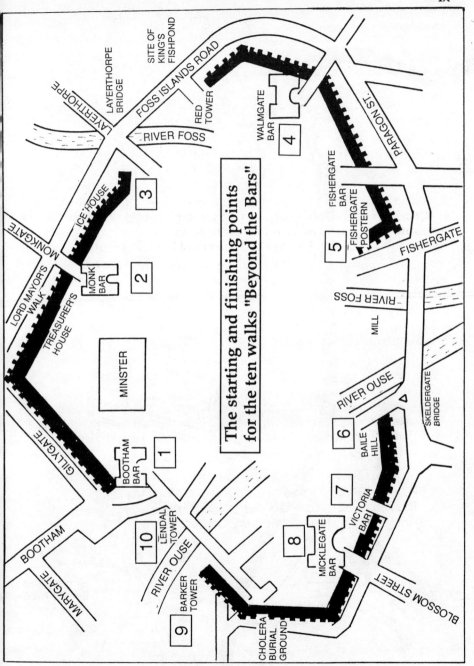

The starting and finishing points for the ten walks "Beyond the Bars"

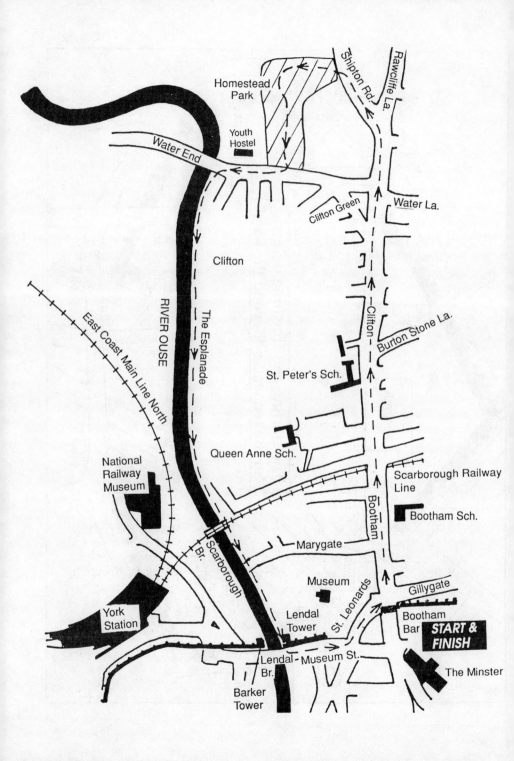

1
In Search of Personalities
BOOTHAM BAR

Bootham Bar — Bootham — Clifton — Shipton Road — Homestead Park —
Water End — The Esplanade — Museum Street — St Leonard's Place —
Bootham Bar.

approx. 2½ miles

STANDING ALMOST EXACTLY on the site of the north-west
gateway of Roman Eboracum, the present Bootham Bar is of
medieval construction when it was known as Galmanlith. The
barbican, said to have been the finest in York, was demolished in 1835
when the inner half of the gate-house was built, replacing a classical facade
of 1719 with a central niche housing a statue of Ebrauk, the legendary
pre-Roman founder of York.

In 1894 George Milburn carved the statues on top of the Bar to replace
the crumbling remains of older statues — probably St John of Beverley, St
William of York, and St Wilfred of Ripon. The present figures show: a
fourteenth century Lord Mayor in official robes carrying a scroll which
reads "Restored 1894"; a mason holding a model of the bar; and a knight
in medieval dress. The coats of arms below, renewed in 1969, show the
Stuart royal arms and on the smaller shields the city arms.

In 1501 an order was made that a hammer be provided here so that
Scottish persons who wished to enter the city should knock first on the
Bar and seek permission from the Lord Mayor, Warden, or Constable, on
pain of imprisonment.

Stretching away from the city is Bootham on the line of a Roman road,
being the main road to the city from the North. Known in 1150 by the old
West Scandinavian name Buthum — "at the booths" — it may have been
a district of humble or temporary dwellings but more probably perpetuates a reference to the fair or market held here in the twelfth century — a
source of dispute for many years between the monks of St Mary's Abbey
and the citizens of York. The abbot claimed that the market belonged to
the Abbey but the civic authorities maintained that all market tolls were
payable to them.

In 1218 the Justices of Assize decided in favour of the citizens but there
was smouldering jealousy and in 1262 a violent affray resulted in several
Abbey servants being killed and a number of houses being burned.

Another legal tribunal secured written undertakings to maintain the peace but the prudent Abbot decided to secure more practical protection than a written piece of parchment.

He obtained permission from Henry II to build a boundary wall around the abbey and this was completed in 1266. The start of the wall is an archway known as Queen Margaret's Gateway or Queen Margaret's Arch, recalling one of the most magnificent pageants the city has ever seen. King Henry VII in 1502 had arranged the marriage by proxy of his eldest daughter, Princess Margaret to King James IV of Scotland. She was then only twelve years old.

Accompanied by a retinue of five hundred consisting of lords and ladies with their servants, she arrived at York in 1503 after being met at Tadcaster by the city sheriffs and an escort of eighty gentlemen. There followed two days of almost continuous ceremonial and feasting before she departed north to her future home having made the famous remark: "How sweetly the bells of York do ring".

A metal plaque here reads:

This gateway was broken through the Abbey Wall July 1503 in honour of the Princess Margaret, daughter of Henry VII who was the guest of the Abbot of St. Mary's for two days on her journey to the North as the Bride of James IV of Scotland.

However some authorities contend that the postern was not made as a convenient exit for Margaret in 1503 but had already been created in 1497 when the Abbot of St Mary's was expecting the king to stay with him while visiting the city.

Two pairs of houses of great historical and architectural interest stand at the corner of Bootham — numbers 15 and 17 on your right and numbers 3 and 5 across in Gillygate. Thomas Wolstenholme, carver and maker of architectural ornaments in composition built them as he related in his will dated 1800.

"I . . . from the beneficence of my Creator have been blessed with Health and Genius in the year 1790 to purchase of Mr John Hudson a freehold estate situated at the corner of Bootham and Gillygate in the parish of St Giles . . . upon part of which premises in the year 1797 I built two houses fronting into Gillygate and also in the year 1799 erected a small house facing into Bootham . . . "

He left number 5 to his daughter, and his own residence at number 3 passed to his youngest brother Francis who was to succeed to the business

Bust of Mary Wandesford.

"in Composition, Ornaments, Carving and Gilding, with all the Stock in hand, moulds, drawing tools, books (etc) . . . in the shops" at the King's Manor or elsewhere.

On the left is the White Horse pub with the date AD1895 inscribed in the underside stone of a projecting second floor bay window, whilst surmounting the eaves are some curious ornate metal finials.

Opposite is The Exhibition pub which boasts a priest hole on the top floor and, reputedly, a friendly poltergeist in the bar!

The Abbey Wall can be seen behind shops on the left hand side of Bootham before it reaches St Mary's Tower and continues down Marygate to the river.

On the right stands an almshouse built in 1739/43 for "ten poor gentlewomen who have never been married, of the Church of England, who shall retire from the hurry and noise of the world into a Religious House or Protestant Retirement, " which was endowed by the Hon. Mary Wandesford in 1725. Her bust can be seen on a pedestal on the outsize pediment over the three central bays. It was also known as the "Old Maid's Hospital".

Master builder Robert Clough apparently built number 33 as a speculative venture in 1754 but it is significant as the home of astronomers Nathaniel Pigott and his son Edward, who discovered Pigott's Comet while living here in 1783. In contributions to the Royal Society, Edward Pigott pays tribute to his contemporary and collaborator John Goodricke. In one paper dated "Bootham, York, March 16th, 1786" he writes of "our observatory, which is in Bootham about 400 or 500 yards N. W. of the Minster ".

As you walk forward you will see a number of fine Georgian town houses like number 39 on your right which displays a metal Sun emblem with the number 271173. This is one of the old Insurance emblems, relics of the early days of fire insurance when the companies felt it desirable to identify the properties 'covered' by them in case their private fire brigades should extinguish the wrong fire. The insurance companies disbanded their own brigades in 1875 when York Corporation took over fire-fighting responsibility. Two were Yorkshire Fire and Life Insurance Co., formed in 1824 with an engine house in New Street and the York and North of England Assurance Co. with an engine house in Blake Street. The Yorkshire eventually merged with General Accident Fire and Life Assurance in 1967 and in 1844 the York and North of England became part of Standard Life Insurance.

Outside number 49 is a plaque which reads:

> Joseph Rowntree 1836-1925
> In this house lived a man whose life was to exercise a profound influence upon a City of which he became in 1911 an Honorary Freeman.
> A pioneer of research and reform in social policy and industrial relations, he became chairman of the Company which bears his name and established three Trusts which seek to continue his work through the generous resources he gave to them.

Only a few steps brings you to number 51, the finest late Georgian house in the city. Built about 1800 by Peter Atkinson, senior, for Sir Richard Vanden Bemple Johnstone, it has a Doric portico to the door and an Ionic window surround above.

Born at number 54 on your left on 21 February 1907 was the poet W. H. Auden.

Further along on your right is Bootham Park Mental Hospital built from plans prepared by York's famous architect John Carr and opened on 1 November 1777. The little gate-house sports a colourful example of the five lions used as the city arms. The hospital grounds were the setting for about sixty years from 1859 of the Grand Yorkshire Gala. Beginning as a flower show, it quickly developed into a three-day festival with balloon ascents and firework displays which attracted thousands of visitors who came on railway excursions.

At the June 1911 event the main attraction was the celebrated French balloonist Monsieur August Gondron who took people aloft in his tethered balloon for two shillings and sixpence (12½ pence). Eight people were returning from a trip with his assistant Mister Limery when the cable snapped "causing Mr Limery and his passengers to accelerate with terrific force into the clouds."

When Limery tried to vent off gas from the balloon to rectify the situation the valve release cable also snapped. Courageously he climbed up through the netting supporting the passenger basket and released enough gas for the balloon to descend, but it was two hours later before it landed ten miles away near Elvington and miraculously all the passengers escaped with only scratches and bruises.

In January 1988 a £5,000 water garden with pergola, plant-covered walkway, decorative paving and a fish pond, was officially opened here. Opposite, about where the street of St Mary's now stands on your left, was another popular leisure venue throughout the eighteenth and nineteenth centuries, known as the Cockpit House. An eighteenth century writer describes it as "a handsome assembly-room by a beautiful bowling green" and about 1727 one of York's early companies of strolling players — "Mr Thomas Keegan's Comedians" — gave occasional performances here, their reception being so favourable that Keegan built himself a theatre in the Minster Yard.

Thirty years later it was the scene of much rioting because of public resentment at what was regarded as the oppressive nature of the Militia Act of 1757. This had been passed to facilitate the enlistment of 32,000 men aged 18 to 45 chosen by lot to serve for three years, and each county was required to furnish a quota.

On 15 September a meeting was arranged between citizens and the lieutenants of the Militia for the Wapentake of Bulmer in the Cockpit House. The lieutenants did not turn up so the yeomen and farmers drank all the liquor in the house and then set about gutting it before finally pulling it down. No sooner had this been accomplished than they did the same to another house on the opposite side of Bootham. The Lord Mayor and High Sheriff had to personally intervene to disperse the mob and at the following Assizes many rioters were fined whilst George Thurloo was convicted of being a ringleader and sentenced to death, but this was afterwards commuted to transportation for life.

Some reconstruction must have taken place because, in 1804, the gamblers were gathered for cock fighting with thirty-one cocks, the first pair being "on the sod" at ten-thirty. However, by 1854 the Cock Pit was being described as "a rather unsightly structure" and it was finally demolished before the construction of St Mary's.

As you go forward the road now crosses the York to Scarborough railway line as Bootham gives way to Clifton. This line was one of the creations of George Hudson, given the title of 'Railway King' by the Reverend Sydney Smith.

When York was joined to Darlington on 4 January 1841 by the Great North of England Railway its chairman, George Hudson persuaded his board of directors to agree to Robert Stephenson surveying a route from

Ingram's Hospital

York to Scarborough.

The implication of the survey passed largely unnoticed except by one George Knowles who struck out at the scheme in stylistic prose in a pamphlet sold for sixpence. Amongst his objections was that "carrying the line of the railroad so very near the turnpike road is not very courteous to the female part of our townspeople; should a woman on horseback be overtaken by a railway train she has no chance of escape crossing a railroad at right angles."

Undeterred, George Hudson raised the £260,000 needed for the project by an issue of shares at £25 each, and late in 1843 the directors applied to Parliament for an Act authorising construction of the line which opened two years later.

On your left is Ingram's Hospital for ten poor widows, erected and endowed in 1640 by Sir Arthur Ingram who was High Sheriff of the county in 1619. It is ironical that Sir Arthur should be remembered for a generous action because in reality he was an unscrupulous financier who made a huge private fortune from usury, farming monopolies for the crown, and speculation in land. He used his wealth to buy public office and became the greatest landowner in the county.

Early in 1630 a building plot for the almshouses which consisted of a college with a garden and an acre of land was bought for £50 from Thomas Sandwich of St Mary Gate. The Norman doorway was taken from the partially ruined Holy Trinity Church in Micklegate, the complete arch being bought in October 1630 for thirteen shillings and fourpence (67p). In 1957 the almshouses were converted into four flats.

Opposite is the ten-bedroomed luxury Churchill Hotel opened in 1986 after a £250,000 face-lift. Its showpiece is a dazzling chandelier hanging over the main lobby which needed six men to install. The largest bedroom is the Prince of Wales suite where the future King Edward VII spent a night in 1897. Formerly called Record House, it was built about 1827 for Mrs Barbara Aston Nelson and was described as "a mansion and pleasure grounds" in the first Rate Assessment of 1837. Between 1875 and 1879 it was run as a school for young ladies and was known as Bootham House, but by 1889 it had become Government House and was occupied by Major General Charles Frederick T Daniell C.B. It remained in Government hands passing through various departments until it was closed down in 1984.

Immediately beyond Ingram's Hospital on your left is Queen Anne's Road, constructed about 1895. There have been six English Queens who have borne this name but only two have even the slightest connection of any kind with York. Anne Nevill, the wife of Richard III, accompanied her husband in his triumphal progress through the city in the autumn of 1843 but certainly never did anything to associate her own personality with the city; and Anne of Denmark, the consort of James I, stayed in York for only four days in June 1603 as she was on her way to join her husband in London.

Ten years or so after the road came into existence the first York Secondary School for Girls was built at its southern end on land which had been pasture from time immemorial. When another school was opened in the city it became necessary to distinguish the former and because of the access it was officially named Queen Anne's School.

After passing on your right the White House, which is the home of the

Sundial at St Peter's School

Royal Commission for Historical Monuments, the road is spanned by a footbridge designed by C. R. Thorpe in 1966. This links with the dignified and extensive buildings which have been the home of St Peter's School since 18 October 1844. In 1836 a three-acre site was offered by Earl de Grey for use as a school. A group of businessmen, including George Hudson, commissioned York architect John Harper to design and supervise the construction of the Proprietary school and the Gothic structure started in 1837 was opened on 1 August 1838 as a boarding school for boys. But St Peter's School founded in 1557 and housed in Minster Yard was short of pupils so the two merged and united on the present site. The most famous of its pupils — commemorated by a plaque there — was Guy Fawkes who once owned quite a lot of land hereabouts.

Born in 1570, Guye, son of Edward Fawxe, Registrar of the Consistory Court of York, was educated at St Peter's before it moved to its present site. He became a Catholic sometime before 1591, went to the Netherlands to join the Spanish Army in their fight against Protestants in Flanders, and changed his name to Guido Fawkes. He was introduced to the gunpowder plotters by John Wright whom he had known at school. Fawkes' particular responsibility was to make preparations for the exploding of thirty-six barrels of gunpowder beneath the House of Lords. But he was caught and taken before King James at 4.00am on 5 November 1605. After some persuasive torture he betrayed the other conspirators. They were all hanged, drawn and quartered on 30 January 1606. The following day he suffered the same fate.

Notice near the school exit the ornate sundial with armorial shields in grey stone whilst across the road St Peter's Grove has dark-red brick houses of the 1880s with terra-cotta sunflowers.

A little further forward on the right is Burton Stone Lane which in the Middle Ages marked the boundary within which the "Mayor and Commonalty of the City of York" exercised jurisdiction. In the days of the Plantagenets and Tudors it was the custom of the Lord Mayor, Sheriff and Aldermen to review and take leave here of the levies which the city raised to aid the king in his wars against the Scots. These levies were usually commanded by the Lord Mayor's esquires, predecessors of the modern civic functionaries, the sword and mace bearers.

One such occasion arose in 1482 when a serious dispute developed between England and Scotland resulting in urgent preparations for war being made on both sides of the border. Richard, Duke of Gloucester, was appointed by his brother, King Edward IV, to lead the English forces. A company for the Duke's army was levied in York, and assembled at the Magdalene

Decoration on house in St Peter's Road

chapel preparatory to marching. Instead of marching, however, the soldiers went on strike.

The city council had arranged to provide "a troop of six score archers", and that "every sougeor" should have sixpence a day, be engaged for twenty-eight days, and be paid fourteen days' pay in advance; but when the men had this amount tendered to them "they said plainly that they would have 'hoyll waghis' for the twenty-eight days, or else they would not go"; and my Lord Mayor and his brethren had to give way to them for fear of hindering the expedition, and so incurring the Duke's displeasure.

However, war was averted and in due course the men marched back to

The Burton Stone, outside the Burton Stone Inn.

York. Then came the day of reckoning. The three ringleaders, who said in their defence that it was declared "by the whole fellowship" that "he who took less than the whole wages should repent it" — in modern parlance, would be a blackleg, and would suffer accordingly — were imprisoned

Nell Gwynne House

for ten days and then were liberated on saying they were "ryght sory", and on finding sureties in a hundred marks for future "gude beiryng". The entire affair provoked much adverse comment amongst the citizens who believed that the "sowghers" had enjoyed a good outing at the citizens' expense.

Enclosed in iron railings in front of the Burton Stone Inn built in 1896 is the base of a medieval wayside cross which stood outside the Hospital of St Mary Magdalene, commonly known as the 'Maudlin Spital', founded before 1481 by John Gysburgh, the precentor of York Minster who died in that year. The house was founded for two chaplains and was more in the nature of a chantry chapel than a hospital, although it was a place of some importance in the Middle Ages because Burton Stone Lane — then Chapel Lane — led directly to the Forest of Galtres and travellers often found hospitality and refreshment here. In 1535 the house was stated to be worth £9.6s.0d. The stone also recalls the fact that in 1604 there was a violent outbreak of plague in the city and 3,512 people are said to have died from it. At stone crosses erected on all main roads approaching the city farmers displayed provisions for sale without entering the city.

A little way past is the old Manor House, known as Nell Gwynne's House, with 'Dutch' gables and rusticated front with projecting windows like oriels.

Immediately ahead, covering nearly two acres, is Clifton Green which once boasted a maypole and a horse pond where the cattle trough now stands.

And in the seventeenth century there stood in the vicinity — probably on the site of The Old Grey Mare — an inn called The Maypole which was the setting for two notable criminal episodes.

On 10 April 1647 two sisters called Elizabeth and Helen Drysdale who had lived at the inn were hanged after being convicted for murdering their sweethearts by putting oxalic acid in their beer. The following year another maid from the inn set fire to the place and it was burned to the ground. She was convicted of arson and hanged on 30 April 1649.

Another celebrity associated with Clifton was the famous prophetess Ursula Southeil better known as Mother Shipton. According to a record of 1842 and map of 1851 she was commemorated by a stone column here. This is said to have been inscribed:

> *Here lies she who never lyed,*
> *Whose skill often has been tried;*
> *Her prophecies shall still survive,*
> *And ever keep her name alive.*

Her father is said to have been no less than the Devil himself and her appearance was scarcely calculated to win a beauty title. Big-boned, goggle-eyed, yellow-skinned, shrivelled and wrinkled, with nose and chin like a nutcracker, holding a mouth with one solitary black tooth, she was unlikely to appeal as a pin-up. Her neck was so distorted that her head was supported by her right shoulder, and her crooked legs ended with feet and toes all turned to the left so that she walked crabwise. To marry such a monstrosity required a man of sterling courage. Toby Shipton, a simple carpenter who lived in the village of the same name about four miles further north, was the brave man who took this fateful step in 1512, and from which she gained her nickname.

Mother Shipton

By then she had become a renowned prophetess who had set all England talking about her visions of the future. She foresaw that "around the world thoughts shall fly, in the twinkling of an eye", and in nautical vein she told everyone that "Iron in the water shall float. As easy as a wooden boat."

Having personally organised the baptism of the disfigured Ursula, and convinced that she had remarkable powers, the Abbot of Beverley decided to pay her a visit and persuade her to give him a peep into the future. She told him: "The mitred peacock shall now begin to plume himself, and his train shall make a great show in the world. He shall want to live at York and shall see it, but shall never come thither — and finally after great misfortune he shall finish at Kingston. " This astonished the worthy Abbot who copied it out before returning to Beverley to solve the puzzle.

The mitred peacock was Thomas Wolsey, Dean of Lincoln and almoner to the King who shortly afterwards conferred upon him the Bishopric of Tourney, France, making him possessor of immense revenues. On the death of Archbishop Bainbridge he was appointed Archbishop of York and the Pope made him a Cardinal. His train consisted of eight hundred servants, many of whom were knights and gentlemen with their children put under him for their education. Wolsey lived in splendour. He insisted his Cardinal's cap should be borne aloft by a person of high rank and when he came to the King's altar he would have it placed on the altar. A lowly priest carried before him a silver rod holding a cross; another priest carried the cross of York even in the diocese of Canterbury, contrary to all ancient rules and laws.

Soon after being made archbishop he had thought of living in York but his duties in London gave him no opportunity. He was ultimately ordered by the King to take up residence at Cawood Castle from which he could see York. Before he could go there and carry out his vow to burn Mother Shipton as a witch he was arrested, stripped of his wealth and taken to Leicester Abbey under the care of Sir William Kingston, Constable of the Tower. He died on 28 November 1530 and so the prophecy was fulfilled.

Before she died in 1561, Ursula went on to make many more predictions including: "Water shall come over Ouse Bridge, and a windmill set upon a tower and an elm tree at every man's door". This was verified by the conducting of water through the streets of York through bored elms, and the water house had a windmill on top that pumped up water from the river.

Go forward towards the trough over at the far corner of the green which was a century old in 1983. Hannah Husband (1827-1913) organised sub-scriptions and herself generously gave fourteen guineas towards the trough which was placed on the site of the former insanitary pond.

A contemporary report in the Yorkshire Gazette of 14 July 1883 proves that the tile canopy over the trough was original to the structure . . .

"A cattle and drinking fountain has been erected at Clifton Green at a cost of £130. The trough is of granite and has been supplied through the Metropolitan Association (the Metropolitan Cattle Drinking Trough Association). A cover has been built over the trough designed by Mr Bellerby, junior, and

erected by Mr Bellerby, senior. It is of oak and is roofed with Staffordshire tiles. The approach is firmly laid with Bradford setts".

Still in place, half hidden under the roof are cast-iron lettered plates which may well be original. Two of them read: "The police are instructed to apprehend anyone playing with or dirtying the water".

Cattle trough in Clifton Green.

Continue forward past the church of St Philip and St James and keep left as Rawcliffe Lane forks away right at Clifton Lodge. After passing the raised gardens in front of Ouse Lea flats turn immediately left to enter Homstead Park administered by Rowntree Memorial Housing Trust. Numerous heather gardens, a rock garden built around a pool, and a tree-lined avenue are just some of the features of this green oasis as you make an anti-clockwise circuit to exit by a gateway into Water End. Turn left for a few yards to get across at the Pelican crossing before turning right past the Clifton Bridge Hotel. The Youth Hostel is on your right as you go along Ouse Cliffe Gardens to Clifton Bridge which spans the River Ouse.

At the corner of Clifton Bridge take the path on the left which slopes down to the river bank. Flood marks painted on the wall are a reminder

Plates inside the trough on Clifton Green.

of some of the city's more serious inundations. One white painted line and the date 29 December 1978 marks the level where the water reached (4.83m) 15 feet 10 inches above summer level but on 6 January 1982 it topped that to settle at (5.06m) 16 feet 7 inches.

River flooding in 1731 caused the postponement and transfer to Knavesmire of racing from Clifton Ings, on the opposite upstream side of the bridge. Earliest records of racing in Yorkshire date from 1633 and give this as the battleground, from 13 September 1709, on which the 4-mile heats were contested. Two days later when four horses contested for a plate worth £10, Mr Welburn's *Button* and Mr Walker's *Milkmaid* "came in so near together, that it could not be decided by the Tryers; and the Riders showing foul-play in running, and afterwards fighting on horseback, the plate was given to Mr Graham" who had entered his grey called *Brisk*.

Clifton Bridge was built after fifty years of argument about plans, petitions, promises, talks and more plans, until the scheme earned the description of 'York's Comic Opera'. The £230,000 six-span concrete structure was eventually opened on 28 October 1963 by the Lord Mayor with the observation that it was the first bridge to span the River Ouse since January 1881.

Walk along the tree-lined towpath beside playing fields which eventually give way to the open grass space which forms part of the city flood protection system. Across it are distant views of the Minster towers. The boathouse of York Canoe Club marks the start of Almery Terrace where the flood walls and special gates are a reminder of the ravages wreaked by the raging river which passes under, as you do, Scarborough Bridge built in 1844 to carry the York and Scarborough railway. This was the first bridge inside the city boundaries besides Ouse Bridge to provide facilities

Church of St Philip and St James, Clifton.

for pedestrians to cross the river. At first the footway was situated in the middle between the up and down lines but in 1874 a section about eight feet wide was built on the south side at a lower level to take pedestrian traffic, as it does today.

You now enter Earlsborough Terrace which is a reminder that all the land adjoining it on your left was once known as Earlsborough, for it was the administrative centre of the province ruled by the Saxon Earls of Northumbria.

The most infamous of the Earls was Tostig, third son of Earl Godwin of Wessex, brother-in-law of King Edward the Confessor, and brother of Harold, the English king who was killed at the Battle of Hastings. Tostig was said to be "a tyrannous and bloodthirsty man and a great raiser of tolls and taxes". We are told discontent with his rule came to a head in 1064 when in his own chamber he treacherously slaughtered two noblemen who had come to confer with him under a sworn safe-conduct. Open insurrection broke out in October 1065 when a strong force of Northumbrians rifled his mansion and scattered his household at Earlsborough during which they drowned two hundred of his servants in the River Ouse *extra muros civitatis* — "outside the walls of the city". Pass in front of Esplanade Court to reach the cobbled wharf at the foot of Marygate.

The Abbot of St Mary's had the honour of being mitred and had a seat in Parliament, for which reason he bore the title of Lord Abbot. He also had several country houses, one of which was at Overton some three miles up river so He frequently departed from here in his state barge with his grand and numerous retinue.

The long dispute between city and abbey erupted again in 1377 when the mayor claimed a right of way from the river through Marygate to Bootham. The bursar of the abbey disputed the claim and had a ditch dug across Marygate to prevent traffic passing. At the same time he seized the rudder of a ship belonging to John de Roucliff that was awaiting discharge at Marygate landing, to assert his claim that the landing was the private

Barge at Marygate Landing

property of the abbey and no one else had the right to moor vessels there. The city won the resulting lawsuit and the abbey was compelled to fill in the ditch and restore the road.

Two years later, in May, William Mynne fell from the mast of a ship here and was rescued in a dying condition. His devout rescuers, hoping that the Blessed Virgin might work a miracle on his behalf, rushed him through the great gate of the abbey into a chapel and laid him before the altar. Immediately they got him there he died and his soul was commended to God.

A century ago the river was busy with barges trading to Boroughbridge and Ripon as well as weekly market boats serving upriver villages. In 1322 when King Edward II defeated the Earl of Lancaster's rebellion at Boroughbridge, he and his fellow captives were brought down the river to York on their way to Pontefract to be beheaded.

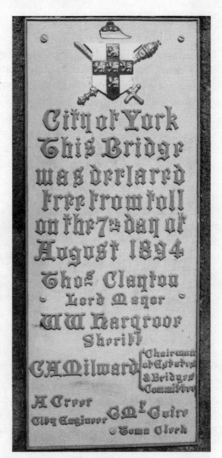

Plaque on Lendal Bridge

Continue along the Esplanade towards the end of which mounted in the pavement beside some railings on the right is a large stone inscribed:

The River bank between this point and Scarborough Bridge was paved and restored in 1966 by the YORK CORPORATION. This improvement was made possible by the JOSEPH ROWNTREE MEMORIAL TRUST and the YORK CIVIC TRUST. The design by H. F. CLARK PPILA AInstPA was included in his RIVER OUSE SURVEY REPORT commissioned by the two TRUSTS and presented to the City in 1965.

Ahead is Lendal Bridge, designed by Thomas Page, engineer of Westminster Bridge, and opened on 8 January 1863 to replace a ferry run by John Leeman since 1851. Four months later he was compensated for his loss of business with £15 together with a horse and cart. Work began in 1860 but after a year the whole lot fell into the river, killing five men. To celebrate the opening the Lord Mayor entertained 120 guests at the Mansion House, while the men who had worked on the structure sat down to their dinner in the "outer wool shed" adjoining the cattle market.

Bear left before some steps and walk up the cobbled slope which used to be called Lendal Hill and was originally St Leonard's Hill, leading directly from the arched entrance of the ancient Hospital of St Leonard to the river where the wharf or landing belonging to the hospital formerly stood. In the reign of Henry V when Henry, Lord Scrope of Masham, who had a house in the churchyard of St Martin, Coney Street, was convicted of treason and beheaded, it was the duty of the Lord Mayor of York to take possession of the property of the traitor found within his jurisdiction, which was forfeited to the Crown. Among other things seized was a certain ship laden with goods belonging to the Lord Scrope which was moored *"apud St Leonard Lendyngs in aqua de Use"*.

At the top of the slope you join Museum Street which was originally a lane leading from Blake Street along the eastern boundary wall of St Leonard's Hospital and was very narrow and inconvenient until about 1782 when it was widened by removing portions of the hospital buildings and several small houses were built on the line of the boundary wall. These were taken down in 1846.

This street has enjoyed an extraordinary variety of names. In the reign of Henry VI a charter describes two tenements near St Leonard's Hospital in Ficteles Lane. At a later period this seems to have been corrupted to Footless Lane, a name used in the reign of James I and on a map as late as 1766. Since then it has been called Finkle Street, and more recently Back Lendal was thought to be an appropriate name before it acquired its present Museum Street.

Go forward to the traffic lights where you turn left into St Leonard's Place to return to Bootham Bar.

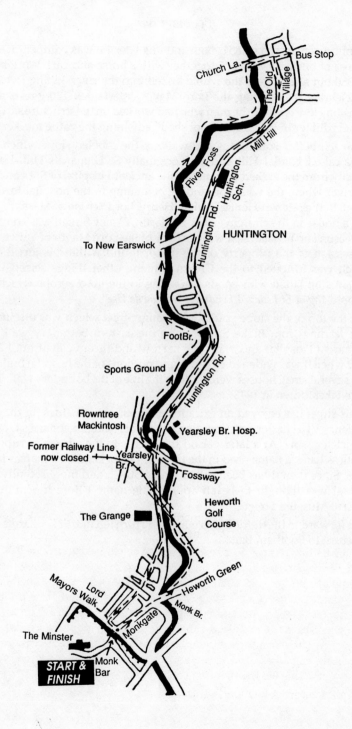

2

The Enigma of the River
MONK BAR

Monk Bar — Monkgate — Foss Walk — Church Lane —
Huntington Old Village — Mill Hill — Huntington Road —
Grove Terrace Lane — Groves Lane — Lord Mayor's Walk — Monk Bar.

7 miles (or 3½ miles if returning by bus from Huntington)

ORIGINALLY CALLED MONKGATE BAR, possibly after a monastery anciently located in the vicinity, Monk Bar replaced an earlier Roman gateway near the Treasurer's House in 1330 because the clergy objected to a main road running through their precinct. It is the loftiest — 63 feet high — and strongest of the medieval gateways, having been constructed as a self-contained fortress with every floor defensible even if others were captured. The fine vaulted arch with battlemented gallery enabled soldiers to drop missiles on attackers if entrance was gained through the barbican, which was demolished in 1825. The only working portcullis in the city can still be seen here. The coats of arms below decorated canopies are the Plantagenet royal arms (before the nineteenth century restoration they bore the many fleurs-de-lys of Edward III or Richard II) and the arms of the city of York. The six figures of wild men grasping boulders are probably seventeenth century replacements of earlier carvings.

As long ago as 1070 Monkgate was known as Munecagate and had become Munkgate by 1154 but nobody seems to know how the name arose.

Walk out of the gate and immediately on your left is Monk Bar Court which was formerly Elbow Lane.

Set back on your right, sandwiched between the walls and the Bay Horse Inn, is a rare Ice House of the kind which were in common use during the eighteenth and nineteenth centuries. They were associated generally with large houses and were used to store ice obtained from frozen ponds and rivers during the winter months for use in the house during the summer. They were usually in the form of a deep brick lined pit with a dome roof above ground surmounted by soil and having an enclosed access passage. The ice was packed between layers of straw and could be stored for up to two years. This Ice House was probably built around 1800.

Walk forward a few yards and on your left is a road with the puzzling

Ice House near Monk Bar

name of Lord Mayor's Walk. In 1736 we are told "Lord Mayor's Walk is a long broad walk which was planted with elms on both sides in 1718". This official planting — which may be the earliest record of a deliberate plan to beautify the streets — suggests that it was the intention to create a fashionable promenade such as was established twelve years later in the formation of New Walk along the River Ouse bank.

On the corner is an area of turf, trees and gravestones which is all that remains of the church of St Maurice. A church existed here well before 1240 when Archbishop Walter de Grey made various adjustments in its revenues, and in 1428 it was among the poorest of York parishes. In 1585 the parish was joined to Holy Trinity, Goodramgate but, as one chronicler noted with some surprise, "Notwithstanding its annexation to Holy Trinity it is still kept up, and divine service celebrated there; the only instance of this kind in or about the city". Development of the locality as a residential district resulted in a new church being built in 1877/8 but this was demolished in 1966/7.

Among the memorials is one "To the Memory of George Mason, Perpetual Overseer and Collector of this Parish who departed this life February 2nd 1859 aged 62 years. This stone is erected by his only sons Joseph and George.

> *Green be the Turf above thee, Friend of our Youthful days*
> *None knew thee, but to love thee, none named thee but to*
> *praise."*

Immediately opposite is St Maurice's Road which back in 1373 was Barker Hill and continued to be so until about 1891. Its medieval name indicates that barkers or tanners carried on their trade here as well as within the city at Tanner Row.

As you walk down Monkgate you pass on your left the Tap and Spile public house, named after the tap inserted into a beer barrel and the ventilation pegs, but formerly the Black Horse Hotel of 1897 as is indicated by the colourful bas-relief on the front.

On your right is No 44 where lived one of York's most famous citizens — the 'Railway King', George Hudson. Born at Howsham on 10 March 1800, son of a yeoman, Hudson was a linen draper, having become apprenticed in 1815 to drapers Bell & Nicholson in College Street. By 1821 he was profit sharing in the business, became a partner in 1828 and married the boss's daughter.

In 1833 he started promoting railways and eventually became chairman of some of the most important railway companies in the kingdom. He was elected an Alderman of York on 31 December 1835, Lord Mayor 1837/9 and 1846/7, and also served as Member of Parliament for Sunderland from 1845 to 1849.

Hudson inherited the property in 1827 from his uncle Matthew Bottrill who, in 1776, had taken out fire insurance on the old house described as "brick built and tiled" for £300. In the seventeenth century it had been owned by a coverlet weaver, than a cordwainer, followed in the eighteenth century by an apothecary who sold it to a yeoman whose son-in-law Joseph Beckett was a butter-weigher. In 1760 Beckett's widow disposed of the house to the painter Thomas Beckwith (1731-86) who was also a pioneering archaeologist. The house was sold by Beckwith's son, a doctor of medicine, to Bottrill who was described as a gentleman.

Legend has it that the railway network was the creation of 'poor-boy-made-good' Hudson living up to a promise to "mak all t'railways cum to York" but who was caught out in dubious dealings on the stock exchange. Before he started the railway business, however, he was already very wealthy — through a massive £30,000 he inherited in mysterious circumstances. From contemporary accounts it appears that he sat for hours at the death-bed of affluent uncle Matthew Botterill and virtually guided his hand to make a will in Hudson's favour.

Hudson appears to have taken over the nearly bankrupt North Midland Railway and kept shareholders happy by paying dividends out of their own capital. As chairman of the York and Newcastle Railway Company he sanctioned the issue of new guaranteed stock to buy Great North of England Railway shares at the lowest market prices. In sole control of the deal he bought more than £130,000 worth of the stock and sold it to his own company at an inflated price, pocketing the profits. Other dubious dealings were discovered and he was obliged to leave the country for a time.

York, scandalised, removed his portrait from the Mansion House and renamed Hudson Street as Railway Street — the "Railway King" who left the rails was expunged. *Punch* had a cartoon of Hudson tilting off the track with smoke billowing from his head. The street name was restored to mark the centenary of his death and his portrait returned to the Mansion House where his prosperously jowled features look down with the pride that preceded a notorious fall.

He died in London on 14 December 1871, aged 71, and is buried in the family grave at Scrayingham near Malton.

Also on the right is the large building which used to be York County Hospital, established in 1740 thanks to an original donation of £500 from Lady Elizabeth Hastings. The original building stood close to Monkgate, having a frontage of seventy-five feet, but a larger establishment costing £11,000 was built in 1849/51 to designs of J.B. and W Atkinson on land which formed part of the hospital's original estate, and was opened the following year.

The first honorary surgeon was Francis Drake, the famous York historian. In 1747 he was deprived of his office for refusing to take the oath of fealty to the Government at the time of the '45 rebellion. He was a strong Tory with Jacobite sympathy like his gynaecologist colleague Dr John Burton. In pursuit of their antiquarian interests the two men set out together to survey " some Roman Curiosities, found in a Field near Millington, on the Wolds". As Drake recorded, "whilst we were upon the Spot & directing this Survey, in the Year 1745, a Year in which the House of Stewart again attempted to recover the British Crown, some People observing us, gave Information at York, that we were marking out a Camp in the Wolds; which had like to have occasioned us some Trouble to contradict."

Brigardier Gerard inn sign.

On your left is The John Petty Memorial Church of red brick which serves Methodists.

All the land hereabouts was formerly within the boundaries of the Forest of Galtres right up to the city walls. How dense it was can only be a matter of conjecture but it is certain that around six hundred years ago a portion of forest land lying on your left had been cleared and enclosed. This was called Paynly Crofts. In 1484 it was claimed that this enclosure belonged to the Abbot and monastery of St Mary's and so the citizens of York had no rights of pasture in it, as they had in the neighbouring "half-year" lands

Monk Bridge over the River Foss.

(i.e. rented for six month periods). The word "Crofts" has been softened over time to become "Groves" while "Paynly" has also been modified to become today's Penley's Grove Street. The *Clifton Book of Record* in 1741 officially refers to it as "Penley Crofts" and in 1688, in a more colloquial style speaks of "The Groves" which clearly shows the process of evolution.

Swinging from the large building which dominates the corner where Foss Bank joins from the right is the colourful pub sign of the Brigadier Gerard — not a military officer but a famous racehorse.

In August 1972 Queen Elizabeth II came to watch the racing at York — the first reigning monarch to do so since Charles I, nearly three hundred and forty years previously. And challenging for the first Benson and Hedges Gold Cup was *Brigadier Gerard*. Victor in all his seventeen races and voted Horse of the Year, *Brigadier Gerard* ridden by Joe Mercer faced major protagonists in *Roberto* and *Reingold*. They had finished respectively first and second in the Derby but *Roberto* had only managed twelfth place out of fourteen runners in the Irish Sweeps Derby. After a great race *Roberto* emerged the victor.

Noticeable as a roundabout is Monk Bridge which has been a crossing point of the River Foss for many centuries and in 1540 had five arches. The name is said to be derived from monks who established the small hospital of St Loy for lepers just across the bridge in early medieval times, although one historian claims it was "a house for the entertainment of poor strangers and pilgrims." The date of its establishment is unknown but a bequest was made to it in 1396. And in 1428 a will was proved of "William Manning, Lazar, of the House of Monk Bridge, York." During the siege of 1644 the bridge was deliberately broken down so that the city could be better defended from the Parliamentarians. For the next fifteen years the public had to rely on a temporary wooden structure until a replacement could be erected. Rebuilding took place in 1794 and widening was carried out in 1924/6.

Cross forward to go over the bridge which carries the Scarborough Road and pass through a small blue iron gate on your left to join a path through the little bit of park along the bank of the River Foss.

Mallard ducks find this a happy home and are easily recognised. The drake is well known for his bright glossy green head, white neck band, chestnut breast, grey body and black and white tail. The duck is much duller; she has feathers streaked in browns and creams so that she is well hidden when sitting on the nest. Both birds have a bright patch of purple on each wing; it is bordered with black and white stripes and called the speculum, being most obvious when seen in flight.

Coots too can be seen here restlessly swimming about looking for food. They are black, rounded birds with an obvious white front to the head and white bills, making them unmistakeable. Coots mainly eat waterweeds but will also take insects, fish, worms, molluscs,and come out on to the banks to graze on grass. Out of the water their large greenish feet can be seen, with lobes of skin along the toes to help in swimming.

The river drains over thirty thousand acres and has its source at Pond Head or Oulston Reservoir about a mile west of Yearsley before following a tortuous 21-mile course to join the River Ouse at York. The Foss Navigation Company canalised the southern section of the river between 1794 and 1805.

The Foss Navigation Company was formed to "facilitate the conveyance of all sorts of Merchandise, and of Coal, Lime, Manure, Gravel, Timber, and materials for building, between the said City (York) and several Towns, Villages, and Places in the said North Riding." And so it did for forty-eight years until purchased by York Corporation for £4,000 in 1853. But the opening of the Scarborough railway line in 1845 had spelt disaster and the Foss gained the dubious distinction of becoming the first navigation to succumb to railway competition.

The Foss was left to silt up as pigsty. Stables, ash pits, and privies discharged into the river. It was like a "stagnant pond" in parts of the city said Mr Creer, York's engineer in 1894. Since that time much has been done and continues to be done to improve it. At least floating masses of rotting vegetation provide welcome nesting places for the little grebe and dabchick. Shy, retiring birds, diving quickly below the water surface when disturbed, they can be watched if approached quietly, but they can be more easily heard in Spring. They have a loud high-pitched laughing call which the male and female often sing as a duet. In the later Summer the adults can be seem feeding the young, constantly diving and fetching up food for them.

The River Foss, upstream from Monk Bridge.

Upstream from Monk Bridge, St Mary's Abbey had land on which stood three windmills with a water-mill on the river. The site of this place is probably retained in the name of the large house 'The Grange' on Huntington Road whose bulk you can see on your left.

Go under the railway bridge and follow the tree-lined path before going around King George VI playing fields. Veer right at the far end to climb some stone steps. Pass between two commemorative gate-posts on the opposite side of which you will find one has a stone lettered George V AD 1910-1936 with a lion holding a heraldic shield whilst the other is inscribed King Georges Field with a unicorn and shield. Cross Fossway and turn left to a set of traffic lights and cross Huntington Road where you turn right and almost immediately left down some steps to rejoin the river-side path on the opposite bank which continues past the former Yearsley Lock towards Haxby Road.

The Lock Keeper's cottage at Yearsley Bridge was offered to the Watch Committee in 1882 as a residence for a Police Constable at a rent of one shilling a week. But the constable, in addition to his normal duties, was required to operate the sluices on the lock and attend to the swans and baths!

This was necessary because the Corporation, after an Act of 1859 closing the navigation outside the city boundaries, converted a stretch of river near Yearsley Bridge into an open air swimming bath at a cost of £300. For a distance of at least one hundred yards the bed of the river was paved. The depth varied from three feet on the west bank to six feet in the middle. Dressing sheds were erected on the west bank and an attendant was provided for safety and order reasons. No charges were made, and this swimming place in the Foss was used from 1859 until 1935.

Opposite is the factory and headquarters of Rowntrees whose products include *Kit Kat, Aero, Smarties, Black Magic, Polo,* and *After Eight Mints,* amongst others. *Kit Kat* is sold in over a hundred countries and some forty are said to be eaten in Britain every second!

Joseph Rowntree was born on 24 May 1836 at his father's shop in Pavement (between Fossgate and Piccadilly) where he served his apprenticeship. He then worked for a wholesale grocer in London to gain more experience, but on the death of his father in 1859 he undertook, with his brother John, responsibility for the business. He was then 23 years old.

In 1868 he left the Pavement shop and joined his younger brother Henry Isaac who now owned a "Cocoa, Chocolate, and Chicory Works" at Tanners Moat down by the River Ouse. This business was derived from a groceries shop opened by a Quaker called Mary Tuke, becoming a tea and coffee dealers under the name of William Tuke & Sons which Henry Isaac acquired in 1859.

In 1879 the total Rowntree staff numbered a hundred, including three clerks and six travelling salesmen. Claude Gaget, a Frenchman, was put in charge of the manufacture of pastilles and gums which soon became one of Rowntrees most popular lines.

Henry Isaac died in 1883 and Joseph's became the guiding hand culminating in land being acquired off Haxby Road on the outskirts of the city where the firm now manufactures on about 130 acres. In later years he used the fortune he had made to set up three trusts, one of which built the nearby village of New Earswick.

The path winds along beside the river where until half a century ago, before the expansion of housing, you would have been rewarded with frequent sightings of kingfishers, but it is now a rare experience. The kingfisher is the gem of the river, its most striking colour once seen will never be forgotten, an electric blue flash, vivid when seen against the background of dark water or trees. It has a rapid whirring flight and often sits on a waterside perch waiting to plunge into the water for food, returning to the perch to eat. The kingfisher has a very direct flight and will if disturbed fly away at great speed about a foot above the water.

When you reach Haxby Road go up the steps and through the stile in the railings at the Ebor Way and Foss Walk signs. Then proceed for about a hundred yards past the New Earswick sign and the overgrown ashlars and crumbling banks of the old lock with the nature reserve alongside.

Stinging nettles and other varieties are abundant on the bank here. Some people believe that nettle juice is a cure for rheumatism whilst others maintain that if men comb their thinning hair the wrong way each morning with a comb dipped in it they will not go bald! Well within this century, fresh nettles were gathered in May or early June to be fed to poultry and pigs or given to horses in the notion they made the horses frisky and added sheen to their coats. They were also boiled and eaten by humans after being made into a soup or eaten as a vegetable. Aaron Hill tells us:

> *Tender-handed stroke a nettle*
> *And it stings you for your pains.*
> *Grasp it like a man of mettle*
> *And it soft as silk remains.*

Footpath signs direct you around Lock Cottage where the path continues once again along the river bank under a road on the route of the former York to Hull railway line and through New Earswick.

In the words of the Trust Deed, the New Earswick village was built to improve "the condition of the working classes, including not only artisans and mechanics but also shop assistants and clerks, and all persons who earn their living wholly or partially, or earn a small income by the work of their hands or their minds and further include persons having small incomes from invested capital, premiums or other sources, in and around the City of York and elsewhere in Great Britain and Ireland, by the provision of improved dwellings with open spaces and where possible gardens to be enjoyed therewith and the organisations of village communities, with such facilities for the enjoyment of full and healthy lives as the Trustees shall consider desirable"

Stone cross at Huntington.

The first houses were built in 1904 after Joseph Rowntree bought from Lord Hawke of Wiggington for £6,000 some 150 acres of agricultural land to pro-

All Saints Church, Huntington

vide what was one of the first garden villages in England. Raymond Unwin of Letchworth who had trained as an engineer and architect was the creator of spacious houses varying in style and type but usually in blocks of four with rooms facing south and each with a garden and two fruit trees. Set in wide roads, with grass verges planted with trees, they set the pattern for private building estates of the 1920s and 1930s, recognising New Earswick as a pioneer in domestic architecture in the first fifty years of the twentieth century.

Rents were kept to a bare minimum so that the needy, elderly and infirm could afford to live there. The community blossomed and what was once a small village is now nine hundred homes, community centres, sports fields and schools — still run by the Joseph Rowntree Memorial Trust. The Folk Hall is the centre-piece of the village which was built without a pub as a result of the Quaker beliefs of Joseph Rowntree who decreed that no building should be used " for the manufacture, distribution, or sale of beer, wine, spirits or other intoxicating liquor without the consent in writing of all the trustees, or all the trustees but one."

Rowntree & Co. was founded as a limited company in 1897 with Joseph as chairman of the board. The workforce increased dramatically from 1,200 in 1897 to about 4,000 in 1909 and by the 1980s more than 30,000 were employed worldwide. In 1969 the company merged with John Mackintosh & Sons of Halifax, adding *Good News, Quality Street,* and *Rolo* amongst others to the brand names. In 1988 the company was acquired by the Swiss company Nestlé.

Soon you see the spire of All Saints church at Huntington which was rebuilt in 1874 but has a twelfth century doorway and until it was given to Easingwold parish church in August 1981 boasted a fine lychgate dating from 1875. Lychgates were designed as a resting place for coffins during funerals. A most unusual possession of the church is a small pewter font inscribed "Huntington 1823" and a bowl inscribed "Relic of a font 1821 for use in private baptisms". There is also a fine Jacobean pulpit on which are the words "Where there is no vision the people perish". (*Prov., 29, 18*). In 1517, William Appleton, the vicar, left in his will bee-hives to maintain the lamp hanging before the altar of Our Lady in the body of the church.

An earlier church on the site is reputed to have had a lantern tower like All Saints, Pavement to guide travellers through the Forest of Galtres.

Opposite is West Huntington Hall, which now serves as offices, rebuilt by Captain Thomas Dowher before 1857 on the site of an old hall owned by Sir Thomas Ingram in 1629.

The abundance of trees is a reminder that the river was once surrounded by the Forest of Galtres. The name Galtres derives from the Scandinavian, meaning "boar's brushwood". Although Huntington and Earswick had been established in the forest area by Henry II's reign (1154-89), Robert de Skitherby, an Augustinian Friar at Huntington, was, in 1333, collecting alms for making a safe way through a dangerous spot in the Forest of Galtres. Whether the dangers were from wild animals or from outlaws is not known, but clearly the forest sheltered one or other and probably both.

Under the Norman Kings it became a Royal Forest and as such subject to the Forest law of Henry II. In those days when the forest provided building material, fuel, food, and grazing, severe laws were needed to deter folk from poaching on the king's reserve. The Charters of the Forest of the thirteenth century ameliorated these slightly when "none shall henceforth lose life or limb for venison" so it seems likely that the Foss was even more popular with fishermen than it is now.

Turn right to cross the River Foss by the tiny Church Bridge built in 1840 on the site of one recorded in 1402 and to which in 1435 Margaret Darell left "two torches and her best gilded girdle".

At the end of Church Lane on your left is the base of an old stone cross. One theory is that it was one of many similar crosses designated as sales points where farmers left produce and customers placed their money in the hollows which contained herb disinfectant. Some claim it was a butter cross. Others suggest it saw service during the plague in the same way as the one in front of the Burton Stone Inn. (Walk 1)

That the dreaded scourge reached here is evidenced by a letter from Lord Wentworth in York to Viscount Dorchester dated 22 September 1631.

He wrote:

It is full time in my judgement to give your Lord a shortt accompt of our presentt condition in thes parttes, which as it shall seeme good in your better wisedum, may be made knowen to his Majestie, or my Lords of the Counsell in case you would directte us, any thing more to be dun then is allready.

True itt is (that leaving our neighboures of Lancishire and Lincolnshire miserably distressed with the pestilence) that now within thes sixe weeks the infection is cumd to our selves in divers partts of this County, and last of all into this Citty . . .

Againe, on this side, ther is the toune of Rednes, and Armin, both seated upon this river, furiously infected, at the least fourscore howses infected, and a hundreth persons deade within thes five weekes, besides sum four or five little villadges besides; this being brought to us forth of Lincolnshire, as on the other parte it was forth of Lancishire, and of the tow is observed to be much more taking and deadly.

Finally, it was brought heather by a lewde woman who brake forth of Armin, with the sore running upon her, lodged in an outside of the toune and ther ungratiously left itt behinde her; sinc ther are deade in that street sum fourscore persons, and hath not as yet God be praysed gott within the walls, saving in tow howses, forth of which all the dwellers are removed to the Pesthowses; but is broken forth without the walls at tow other ends of the

Clock Cottage.

toune, and into Huntington and Acam, tow little villadges within tow miles of us . . .

As a postscript he added:

Even now they bring me worde of the plague broken forthe in another little toune tow miles of.

On your right is Clock Cottage which derives its name from the clock built into the wall alongside the door. The church records of 1802 mention the provision of a public clock to be the property of the subscribers, the vicar for the time being to act as Trustee and to call a meeting should circumstances require. The cost was £8. 10. 0d. Some thirty-five years ago during renovations an ancient inglenook fireplace over 300 years old and about ten feet wide was discovered as was a bee-hive. Prior to that time Clock Cottage served as a post office.

This is the Old Village and across the road is the Blacksmiths Arms on the site of an ancient smithy. Next to it is Prospect House which is an early eighteenth century unspoiled Queen Anne building with the original doorway.

Huntingdun as it was called in Old English, derives its name from the personal name, Hunta, with the remainder signifying a farmstead. Over the years Huntingdon lands have been held by a variety of owners, one of the most interesting being the Protestant poet Wilfred Holme who inherited the manor in 1522. His anti-clerical outlook and view of nuns is evidenced in his poem on *The Pilgrimage of Grace* in which he writes:

For Dame Nice and dame Wanton, they set in the quire
Cheeping like gosling, and looking on Sir John,
They had rather than fivepence to have him elsewhere,
If one ask how I knowe it, I will ground on this stone,
They are fat, and fayre of fleshe, blond and bone,
And have not receyved the spirit of veritie . . .

The Burrells took the manor after the Holme family and in 1612 it went to Arthur Ingram, who entered into an agreement with the King for disafforesting lands belonging to the manor which fell within the 'Forest of Galtres'. The Ingrams sold it to the Weddell family who were dominant in the village from 1656 to 1859. On the death of Thomas Philip Weddell in 1859 the manor came to his daughter Lady Mary Vyner whose son Robert Charles de Grey Vyner was lord of the manor earlier this century.

Apart from manorial lands a considerable amount of land in Huntington was held by religious houses and possibly by Crown tenants like Agnes Agar. At her death in 1592 she held land of the queen as of her manor of

Huntington free of obligations "by fealty and the payment of one rose in the time of roses".

If you wish to return by bus, turn right and cross the road to the public footpath sign which directs you through Keswick Way to Huntington Road which you cross to reach the bus stop for services back to the city.

Otherwise continue to your right to pass Peartree Close on your left which stands where the White Horse Inn used to be. Records of the Petty Sessions for 1877 reveal that "George Driscombe, Richard Burfield, William Mercer, Joseph Robinson, Fred Hall were all charged with being on licensed premises drinking ale during the prohibited hours on the 11th March. This at the White Horse, Huntington, kept by James Wedgwood. Sergeant Wright also found several other men drinking ginger beer and eating biscuits at the back of the Inn. Fines of 25/- for all the men".

The last house in Old Village, number one on your right, has over the door a Yorkshire Fire plaque with a representation of the Minster and the date 1921.

Bear right along Mill Hill into Huntington Road past St Andrew's Church on your right. Built in 1913 for Rowntree village, it was designed by Edwin Crumbie and enlarged in 1934. Next you pass on your right Link Road to New Earswick on the route of the former York to Hull railway line.

Soon on your right you will see the stork weather-vane surmounting the printing works of William Sessions Ltd. This company traces its history back through a series of Quaker owners to 1811 when William Alexander began to publish books at premises in Castlegate. Born in 1768 of Quaker parents in Suffolk he trained in the corn and flour trade and married Ann Tuke of York. In the nineteenth century when the corn and flour trade collapsed they came to York to take charge of a school and in collaboration with Ann Tuke's brother, Henry, started publishing books. Between 1811 and 1839 he published some 250 and a replica of his business is now displayed in the Castle Museum. Besides his business activities William Alexander was Chamberlain of York and a leader of philanthropic causes. He denounced the appalling conditions under which boy chimney sweeps laboured; worked for the formation of a savings bank; urged the re-assessment of the window tax (he had so many on his own property) and was interested in many local affairs. He was also a prominent and active Quaker. The business was acquired in 1865 by William Sessions — another Quaker, who served an apprenticeship in the grocery business of Joseph Rowntree — and after occupying various premises moved in 1920 to its present green fields site. And in 1954 they printed the story of Joseph Rowntree's Village Trust in a book entitled *One Man's Vision*. The firm has

continued to expand in a wide range of printing work, including spe-
cialised labels. Additional trees have been planted at the back of the
factory to create a nature reserve alongside the River Foss for water-hens
and other wild birds.

As you continue forward on your left you will see a curious building
with cast-iron verandas and a clock tower. This is the old Fever Hospital
begun in 1789 and in use by 1881, subsequently being extended in 1932.
On your right is the former Yearsley Lock before the road crosses the River
Foss and Fossway to rejoin the river on your left.

Grove Terrace inscription.

Somewhat dispiriting and grim is The Grange on your right, built as a
workhouse about 1847. York has had several workhouses over the years.
The city had been ahead of its time in taking up the idea of setting the poor
to work, beginning a cloth making industry in 1567. The intention was to
discourage beggars from entering the city from the surrounding country-
side and to clear up the streets. After an influx of paupers fleeing the Irish
potato famine in 1847, The Guardians of the Poor agreed to build the
300-bed workhouse which eventually became a city institution for the
aged poor with an infirmary which became the Grange Hospital in 1946.
Later still, the name changed to St Mary's Hospital, before it came under
the control of the City Hospital, becoming a listed building in the 1970s.
The grim reminders of workhouse days were wiped out in a £70,000
refurbishment of the remaining four wards in 1980.

Bear right away from the river, on the opposite side of which was a
Roman cemetery, immediately after Emerald Street on your right. Just
before the pavement starts to rise steeply with a white wooden fence turn
sharp right around number 51 into the narrow Grove Terrace Lane which
gives its name and 1824 date in massive letters over the middle house

which faces on to Huntington Road. Partly paved with what are thought to be old Dutch tiles before it crosses Park Grove, it leads across Lowther Street into Bowling Green Lane past Park Crescent. Continue forward crossing Penleys Grove and passing Lockwood Street and Waverley Street on the left before skirting a car park giving a novel view of the Minster over a row of red brick and tile houses as you proceed down Groves Lane — a narrow thoroughfare, insignificant in appearance but which probably shares the antiquity of York's oldest streets. A record of St Maurice's parish boundaries in 1370 speaks several times of 'Goyse Lane' and in 1539 it had become 'Goose Lane'.

Following a direct route in Roman fashion it brings you in about half a mile to Lord Mayor's Walk and the city walls. Here is believed to have stood the *Porta Decumana* in the centre of the north-east wall of the fortress of Eboracum and although no traces of this gateway are now apparent, its foundations are probably there under the existing wall.

Turn left for the few yards back to your starting point at Monkgate Bar.

3

Fish for a King
LAYERTHORPE POSTERN

**Layerthorpe Postern — Foss Bank — Heworth Green —
Heworth Road — Heworth — Beck Lane — Tang Hall Beck —
Melrosegate — Hull Road Park — Green Dykes Lane — Thief Lane —
Heslington Road — Lawrence Street — Foss Islands Road —
Layerthorpe Postern.**

approx. 3½ miles

L AYERTHORPE POSTERN was a massive, embattled, portcullised tower built on the edge of the River Foss, probably with a drawbridge, but it was demolished in 1829. It was probably built in the fourteenth century and was heightened in 1604 to form a house over the passage.

The first mention of its name is in 1070, in the form Legerathorp. As the G at that time had an almost identical sound to our modern Y it would appear that ancient and modern names are almost identical. Some authorities believe that its meaning is associated with the Old Scandinavian word "leir", signifying clay and that it was the "clay village". Support for this suggestion comes from the existence at one time of numerous brick works hereabouts, but another version claims it is derived from "one who lies with a woman".

Layerthorpe Bridge, or Layrthorpe-brig as it was called in 1381, was deliberately broken down to help defend the city in the siege of 1644.

Probably at that time the water level was low because, according to the diary of Sir Henry Slingsby, "a bridge to clap over ye Fosse and store of Hurdles for a storm whereby ye Latern Posterne it was most easy (to cross)". It was restored in 1656, a wooden gangway having done duty in the meantime. Renovation took place in 1829 to the design of Peter Atkinson the younger, at which time the postern was taken down.

With Peaseholme Green behind you, to your immediate left is an area described on old maps as "The Jewbury", a name it still retains.

Historian Drake says that "beyond Larethorpe Bridge is a place at this day called Jewbury quasi jewburgh, which certainly was the district allowed those mercantile people (meaning the Jews) to live in, *extra muros*(outside the walls), and where they might have the advantage of this navigation" (meaning the Foss). He goes on to qualify this area also as a

Jewish burial ground quoting another historian Roger de Hovedon that "King Henry II granted a license to the Jews to have a burial place without the walls of every city".

By the Inquisition taken upon expulsion of Jews from England by King Edward I in the eighteenth year of his reign it is found that the place called "Le Jiwbiry", which then consisted of eight selions or one acre of land on part of which stood a house, was held by the Jews of both York and Lincoln. And in the first year of King Henry IV a grant was made to Robert de Gare of "two messuages of land, two cottages and one croft called Jewbury, in Monkgate, without the suburbs of the city of York".

Before turning diagonally left up Foss Bank to walk alongside the River Foss look down Layerthorpe which until recently boasted on the left only a few yards ahead a Chicory Yard. At the turn of the century this area was the centre of York's chicory industry. In summertime around three hundred acres of delicate blue flowers with blossoms up to two inches in diameter carpeted the fields around Dunnington to the east of the city.

Layerthorpe Bridge over the River Foss

And as an appreciative observer remarked: "Few things in the natural world are more beautiful than the chicory flower". Introduced into Yorkshire in 1839, the industry took a hard knock in 1863 when Gladstone, then Chancellor of the Exchequer, levied a heavy duty on the product.

A deputation of Yorkshire chicory manufacturers was organised to lobby Parliament but only one man was left to confront the Chancellor — Thomas Smith of Layerthorpe, York. He must have put up a convincing defence because the duty was appreciably reduced. Smith's tenacity was probably inspired by the fact that, according to maps of 1892 and 1909, he had chicory works both in Layerthorpe and at the corner of the former Orchard Street, now an off-street car park. So successful was the business that Thomas Smith & Son was still trading according to directories of 1949/50.

Others living in the vicinity were less fortunate as is instanced by relics of former workers houses here. Slum conditions were sufficiently rife for the council in 1932 to lay down that each person living here must have a minimum of forty square feet of living space to himself; that is a space, for instance, eight feet by five, presumably including the person's bed.

Perhaps habits were less than hygienic because by-laws passed in 1888 for the adjacent River Foss included fifty-three things which must not be done. Penalties awaited anyone "who shall throw any animal, dirt, sand, cinders, ashes, stone, rubbish, ballast, smudge, slack, roots, or any other matter whatever into the river".

Although the river now has lots of green water plants and reeds providing a habitat for coots, ducks, moorhens and other birds, it still has more than its share of debris.

Continue forward with the superstore on your left dominated by the bulk of the former York County Hospital until you reach the landscaped corner, with its hebe, cotoneaster, roses, laurel, maple, quince and other shrubbery, on your right at the junction with Monkgate.

On your left is the Brigadier Gerard public house, named after the famous racehorse who won £212,319 in prize money and retired with seventeen wins and one second from eighteen starts. In 1971 he won the Two Thousand Guineas and the Champion Stakes at Newmarket; the St James's Palace Stakes and the Queen Elizabeth II Stakes at Ascot; as well

Foss Bank alongside the River Foss.

as the Sussex Stakes and the Goodwood Mile at Goodwood. He followed this in the following year when he was voted Horse of the Year by racing journalists, by winning the Lockinge Stakes at Newbury; Westbury Stakes, Prince of Wales's Stakes and Eclipse Stakes at Sandown Park; King George VI and Queen Elizabeth Stakes, and Queen Elizabeth II Stakes at Ascot; and the Champion Stakes at Newmarket.

Turn right to cross the River Foss by Monk Bridge. The remnants of the gas works on your right are a reminder that the original York Gas

Company was set up on 30 May 1823 with 640 shares at £25 each. They were taken up by 136 people including many aldermen and clergy. The company was run by a management committee of fifteen who all had four shares at least. It included, unusually in that day, a woman. York Minster seems to have been supplied with gas about 1825 despite stories of the use of gas on the Sabbath day being frowned upon by religious authorities. The area of supply was a two-mile radius of Ouse Bridge though this was later extended to cover 154 square miles within a seven-mile radius of the bridge.

The land beyond Monk Bridge is generally spoken of as Heworth Moor in early records. The village of Heworth is mentioned in Domesday Book as Hewarde and the road is still called Heworth Green. Part of Heworth's commons and pasture were replaced by Monk Stray in 1817 owned by the freemen of Monk Ward.

Heworth Moor appears to have been the site of a skirmish between the Percies and the Nevilles in 1453. Apparently some 5,000 Percy tenants and York craftsmen ambushed a Neville wedding party, including the Earl of Salisbury who was returning to Sheriff Hutton, having married his son to the niece and heiress of Lord Cromwell at Tattersal Castle in Lincolnshire. According to one report "there were altercations and threats and doubtless a fair amount of rough play, but the Nevilles reached home without bloodshed". But another account claims that many men of both parties were "beten, slayne and hurte". Some 710 Percy tenants and York citizens were prosecuted for 'riotous assembly' being described as clad in "jakkies, loricis and salettes* and arrayed for war" but there are no mentions of deaths in the indictments though one man sued for injuries done to him.

Here on Thursday 14 August 1537 the body of Sir Robert Aske of Aughton — the ostensible leader of the uprising known as the Pilgrimage of Grace — was suspended from a gibbet 35 feet high. The Sheriff, supported by his officers and a troop of Light Horsemen read a proclamation which concluded with a warning to all transgressors of the peace. Also, any person found meddling with the body or damaging the gibbet would be put in prison for twenty years.

In 1642 King Charles I withdrew from Parliament after months of dispute and set up his headquarters in York. One hundred and thirty six men were

---

* defensive leather coats, leather corslets and light helmets. This might have indicated that the party was attired for a fracas — or maybe not.

camped on Heworth Moor. In June of that year he summoned all house-holders to the moor where it was said there was a gathering of sixty to eighty thousand people. Attended by many lords and knights as well as a fully armed force of about a thousand cavalry and infantrymen, the king made a speech calling for "the defence of the true religion and of the laws and constitutions of this kingdom".

Plaque on house in Hyrst Grove.

He received a mixed reception as he sat on horseback surveying the crowd. Sir Thomas Fairfax was seen to approach him fearlessly with a petition from the Parliamentarians. Charles well knew it would contain no pleasing message and contemp-tuously waved him aside but a determined Sir Thomas placed the petition on the pommel of the King's saddle before retreating.

War was declared in August 1643 and the city was garrisoned by the Royalists and families from the sur-rounding areas. In 1644 the Parliamentarians besieged York and four hundred men were said to have been billeted in Heworth. Seven windmills were burned on Heworth Moor and Layerthorpe and Monk Bridge destroyed.

And in 1743 one of John Wesley's followers, called John Nelson from Birstall near Wakefield, was con-scripted into the army under old Militia laws and brought to York where he spent all his spare time in open-air preaching. Large crowds flocked to hear him and on Sunday 27 May 1743 it was estimated that he had an audience of nearly six thou-sand on Heworth Moor. In 1746 he was discharged from the army and became a full-time Methodist prea-cher, but on Easter Sunday 1747, when he again preached on Heworth Moor, he was seriously assaulted by a gang of youths. The same evening whilst preaching at Acomb another mob assaulted him and broke two of his ribs — treatment which apparently was not uncommon for Wesleyan preachers in those days.

Turn right up Heworth Green and notice on your left high up on the eaves of the Victorian edifice number 49 at the corner of Hyrst Grove a colourful and ornate plaque bearing the initials of Queen and Consort with the date 1861. Continue forward with the open space of the golf course on your left. Hereabouts was the site of a Roman cemetery. On your right are three-storeyed terrace town houses and the Shoulder of Mutton pub as you pass Cinder Lane and the North of England Girl Guide Headquarters before reaching a junction, once marked by a wooden cross and a pinfold (cattle pound), where Malton Road swings left across Monk Stray. Only a few yards along that road was the toll bar of the York and Scarborough Turnpike Trust.

The *Yorkshire Gazette* of 31 January 1835 reports an accident here that has modern overtones:

"On Thursday evening the Scarborough Mail was overturned on its way to York, on Heworth Moor; a little on this side of the Toll Bar, under the following circumstances. A rabbit cart had broken down and had been left on the road side. When the Mail came up, the horses took fright and bolted to the opposite side of the road so suddenly that the coachman was upset. The passengers on the outside were thrown off clear of the vehicle, on the stray adjoining, and fortunately received no injury. The panels of the coachman were broken, but no other mischief was occasioned, beyond the inconvenience of delay. Great blame attaches to the owner of the rabbit cart in leaving an object on the road during the night so calculated to frighten spirited animals; and we hope that every care will be taken to prevent such carelessness in future, and to reprehend it whenever it does occur".

Stockton Lane is ahead, but before you turn right into Heworth Road spare a glance at the little building on the corner which now serves as a florist's shop. Originally it was a shelter and charging station for the city's pioneering battery electric buses which were operated from 1915 to 1920 on a route from Clifton to Heworth. The Heworth section was replaced by York's only trolleybus route which operated until 1935.

Proceed forward along the tree-lined road with its old cottages past the Nags Head pub and notice the stained floral glass windows of Pear Tree Cottage and Briar Cottage as you head towards Heworth village. The name Heworth is Anglo-Saxon and means "a high enclosure". In pre-Roman times this area was mostly boggy ground with birch and aspen trees so the small settlement was established on the higher ground and is still called Heworth village.

The first York man to become Lord of the Manor of Heworth was Nicholas Langton in 1316 and the family held the manor for the next hundred years. He became Lord Mayor of York and also Keeper of the Archbishop's Palace and Prison in 1322. The manor was bought in 1568 by Elizabeth Kellet, widow of a York corn merchant and it passed to the Thwenge family who lived in the old Manor House — now de-molished.

At the junction with East Parade you will see Heworth church by G.F. Jones 1868/9 built at a cost of £6,436. Sir Trevor Wheler laid the founda-tion stone on 14 September 1867 and the building was consecrated by Archbishop Thompson on Septem-ber 27, 1869. Dedicated to Holy

Holy Trinity Church, Heworth.

Trinity, it is built of yellowish stone and ivy mantled. Over the north porch is the inscription "Let us go into the House of the Lord". It also boasts an eleven hundred-weight bell and a small bell said to have been dug out of a Westmoreland monastery. In the north transept is a geometric window in memory of Charlotte Starkey of Tang Hall, Heworth dated 1879.

After passing Heworth Methodist church on your left and Yew Villa cottage you are besieged by colourful gardens as you head towards the tree-shrouded Walnut Tree inn. In Summer the heavy sweet scent of honeysuckle or woodbine with its slender ivory tubes of flowers tinged with red permeates the air. It is a mute reminder that seventeenth century astrologer-physician Nicholas Culpeper recommended an infusion of the leaves to soothe sore throats and for the relief of "the cramp and convul-sions of the nerves".

Opposite, on the corner of the now Walney Road, was formerly situated

Walnut Tree Inn, Heworth.

the old Manor House in which the Thwenge family lived.

The junction ahead with Hempland Lane marks the end of Heworth village and you should bear right for a few yards past a terrace of eight bungalows along Beck Lane. Cross the stone-walled bridge over Tang Beck before turning sharp right through a green metal gate to walk between the trees along the grassy path which runs beside the little winding stream where numerous ducks make their home. Colourful gardens slope down to the beck from houses on the opposite side.

Leave by another green metal gate at Bad Bargain Lane whose name tells an obvious story. Cross Hall Lane and bear right a few yards past the electricity sub-station before turning left through a green metal gate to follow the path now with the beck on your left and go through a green turnstile gate to enter Melrosegate where you turn left.

You are in the heart of the district known as Tang Hall. The name Tang means 'the meeting of the two becks'. The Tang Hall, the old Manor House, once existed at the rear of where the present Tang Hall Hotel stands in an area between Fourth Avenue and Tang Hall Lane on your left.

In the 1830s James Barber, a York silversmith and Lord of the Manor of

Osbaldwick bought the 'Tang Hall' which was then a Victorian Manor House. He used his land surrounding the house to pasture the horses for his famous coaching business at the Black Swan in Coney Street.

In the 1880s Captain Edward Charles Starkey of the 13th Hussars and Lady Evelyne Starkey lived at this house in Tang Hall. Charles Starkey died there on 12 January 1906 aged 65 and there is a tablet to his memory in Heworth church although he is buried in York Cemetery where his gravestone reveals that his three brothers — Ernest, Richmond and Percival — were all connected with pioneering Australia and died aged respectively 32, 22 and 21 years. Lady Starkey lived on after his death until 1925. Rumour had it that she was rather eccentric and in her later years it was said she shot nails at trespassers on her land. After her death the estate was bought by York City Council who built up the area, naming Starkey Crescent, after its previous owner.

Having turned left continue past Fourth Avenue and walk beside the tree plantation of horse chestnut, laburnum, lime, birch, willow, prunus, hawthorne, and ash. Cross Starkey Crescent.

A slight rise brings you to the junction with Fifth Avenue where you will see on your left the Roman Catholic church dedicated to St Aelred whose name means "noble counsel". In 1932 Bishop Shine selected Aelred as patron saint of the new parish to commemorate his 800th anniversary as a monk at Rievaulx Abbey. Born at Hexham and educated at the Priories of Hexham and Durham, Aelred came to York aged 25. He is commemorated by a statue, probably the only one of him in Yorkshire, on the outside wall above the door. The foundation stone of the church designed by Stephen Simpson was laid on 12 March 1955 and exactly one year to the day Bishop George Brunner blessed and officially opened it.

The church had occupied a hall from 1932 and many of the original congregation were Roman Catholics of Irish origin who had come over at the time of the potato famine. Daily they used to go to work in the sugar beet factory, cattle market, or different chocolate factories. Women were driven in carts, weather permitting, to Lord Derrimore's estate and worked for him in the fields harvesting potatoes, turnips. and chicory for derisory wages.

You now cross the route of the former Derwent Valley Light Railway which in 1913 put down a track after acquiring the land here from the Church Commissioners from a terminus at Layerthorpe to Dunnington and Wheldrake, extending some sixteen miles as far as Cliffe Common close to Selby.

For the first thirteen years the company carried passengers and freight, but as early as 1926 only a mixed freight traffic service was maintained.

Grain, sugar beet, potatoes, coal, petrol and fuel oil, stone, cement, fertilisers, and livestock were transported to the great advantage of farmers and villagers in this particularly rich agricultural area. But the last train ran on 27 September 1981.

On your right is Rawdon Avenue which marks the eastern end of what in 1926 was a huge clay pit. This provided the raw material for millions of bricks needed to fuel the massive house building schemes hereabouts which were needed after the First World War to rehouse people from the slums of Walmgate.

Only a few more yards brings you to Alcuin Avenue on your left. Alcuin is generally thought to have been born at York, then Eoferwic, in AD735. His boyhood was spent here as a pupil of Aelbert, master of the school founded by Archbishop Egbert. Alcuin subsequently became master here as well as custodian of the library which was one of great fame and value through his collection of important manuscripts.

In AD782 Alcuin went to live at the Court of Charlemagne and died at the Abbey of St Martin, Tours in AD804. He was the most famous schoolmaster of his time and the school at York was one of the most celebrated seats of learning in Europe. He was also the first English puzzlist. One of his best known puzzles is:

If 100 bushels of corn were distributed among 100 persons in such a manner that each man received three bushels, each woman two, and each child half a bushel, how many men, women, and children were there?

One of several answers is *5 men, 25 women, and 70 children.*

On your left, and bordering Alcuin Avenue, is Hull Road Park built around Osbaldwick Beck and worthy of a visit to see the rose gardens and colourful beds of flowers laid out with professional expertise. Go through the gate and make a circuit keeping to your right as you go down a short flight of steps to walk alongside the beck with its abundant waterfowl and a stone lion head protruding from the low wall on your left. Turn left around the tennis courts to the bowling green overlooked by the pavilion surmounted by a dovecote and white doves. Bear left to exit at the gate into Alcuin Avenue where you turn left to return to Melrosegate.

Turn left and continue forward across Osbaldwick beck to reach the Hull Road. The bridge was once called Thief Bridge and there was a mill with millpond there.

The Tang Hall area which stretched away to your right had been mostly fields and pasture grounds, originally owned by the Prebend of Fridaythorpe. At the end of the fifteenth century the City succeeded in

Topiary in Thief Lane.

establishing a right to pasture their cows there, and Tang Hall fields became part of the city's pastures after 1525, although it was actually owned by the Ecclesiastical Commissioners from 1490-1830. At the time of a major plague in York in the sixteenth century the cows were taken off Tang Hall fields and plague victims were placed in plague lodges erected here. The Manor House, 'The Tang Hall' which then served as a farm-house, was also pressed into service as a plague lodge.

Cross forward at the traffic lights to climb the gentle rise of Green Dykes Lane. A prehistoric earthwork known as Green Dykes was formerly a district boundary. As a result of a dispute with the vicar of St Lawrence's Church the dikes themselves were in 1456 declared to be in Fulford.

On your left is Barstow Avenue and off Kexby Avenue on the right is Blakeney Place. At the turn of the century a large house stood in its own spacious grounds near the cross-roads ahead. Beyond its massive wrought iron gates there were wide lawns and a wealth of trees and plants with a winding drive that led up to the imposing front door. The house was Garrow Hill and the family who lived in it were called Barstow — hence the name. It was a Miss Barstow who married Baron Orczy and she, the Baroness, was the author of *The Scarlet Pimpernel* which tells the hair-raising adventures of Sir Percy Blakeney who saved aristocrats from the guillotine during the French Revolution.

At the cross roads turn right along Thief Lane at the corner of which, on your right is a garden with an example of the topiarists art — privet columns surmounted by balls. Another garden is devoted entirely to heathers.

Pass The Retreat mental hospital on your left as you descend past the Herdsman's Cottage (No 103) towards Heslington Road. At the terrace of houses numbered 95 to 87 on your left turn right where the sign points to 46/69 Regent Street and follow the pathway alongside the red brick wall until you reach a gateway on your left.

Enter the churchyard of the century-old parish church of St Lawrence, built in 1881 with a spire added in 1893, and so large that it is known as "the Minster without the walls".

In its shadow is the tower of an earlier church dating from 1316 and nearly destroyed in the siege of 1644, before being finally demolished in 1881/3. Local historian Francis Drake recorded in 1736: "The church was laid in ruins like its great neighbour, St Nicholas', and so it remained for over twenty years, when it was restored (1669) and re-edified". By the time he made that observation many of its stones had already been used to make a pavement along Lawrence Street.

Rigg grave and old church tower.

The old church did however provide the setting for a high society wedding on 14 January 1719 when the architect-dramatist Sir John Vanbrugh married Henrietta Maria Yarburgh of Heslington Hall, the Elizabethan mansion which was to form the nucleus of York University in which Vanbrugh's name was given to one of the colleges.

The previous Christmas Day he had written to the Duke of Newcastle, "'tis so bloody cold, I have almost a mind to Marry to keep myself warm".

One relic of the old church, which today plays a vital part in the life of the church, is the fifteenth century font, decorated with bands of carving including devils and monsters' heads. The carved capitals by York sculptor George W Milburn are worth examining for the delights they offer including four owls among ivy leaves, vines, grapes, tendrils, birds, lilies, oak leaves and acorns. The figures on the corbels are painted in bright heraldic colours and a south wall window has the unusual subject of the great teacher Alcuin.

Tam O'Shanter inn sign.

Beside the old tower is the only surviving grave. White and dove-grey marble stands over the vault, the work of York mason William Plows, where the draped urn of the Rigg family is a touching survival and reminder of a nineteenth century tragedy.

On the afternoon of 19 August 1830 Fishergate nursery seedsman John Rigg's family of two daughters and four sons were full of high spirits and entertaining a visitor — Miss Grace Robinson of Ayton near Scarborough. Joined by Thomas Sellers, son of the Falcon Inn landlord, they set off in a rowing boat for an outing on the River Ouse. The exuberant party met a keel coming down river under full sail near Acomb and for some unknown reason collided. The whole party were flung into the water and only two — Thomas Sellers and nine-year-old Jessy Rigg — survived. A stunned public subscribed the monument to commemorate the calamity and beneath it lies 19-year-old Ann, 17-year-old Eliza, 18-year-old Thomas, 16-year-old John, 7-year-old James and

6-year-old Charles. And to keep alive the circumstances of their demise Sheffield poet James Montgomery composed a special epitaph:

Mark the brief story of a summer's day!
At noon, youth, health, and beauty launched away;
Ere eve, death wreck'd the bark, and quench'd their light,
Their parents' home was desolate at night:
Each pass'd alone that gulf that no one can see -
They met next moment in Eternity.
Friend, kinsman, stranger, dost thou ask me where?
See God's right hand, and hope to find him there".

The monument, completed and erected by 15 January 1831, is full of symbolism: carved water and ivy leaves for friendship; classical echoes of the 2,000-year-old tomb of Greek youths at Thysillus.

Over the wall on your left is the Ellen Wilson Hospital built in 1894 by A.S. Ellis of Westminster. Walk forward to leave the churchyard at Lawrence Street where you turn left.

Across the road is the Tam o'Shanter pub. This was originally the name of a drunken farmer in a poem of the same name by Robert Burns. The poem was published in 1791 and tells how Tam interrupts a witches' Sabbath. He is pursued by one of the witches, Cutty Sark, to the Doon river and only just escapes with his life. The witch was named after the

The Red Tower.

short shirt she was wearing. The name tam-o'-shanter was later applied to a bonnet made of wool. There was a horse called *Tam o'Shanter* in the nineteenth century which had considerable success and from the sign-board it would appear that it is from this which the pub takes its name.

The Waggon and Horses, the Rose and Crown and The Queen public houses add a touch of colour with their signboards as you cover the last few yards to Walmgate Bar.

Cross at the traffic lights and turn right up Foss Islands Road — a name which recalls an important phase in York's medieval history. At that time the River Foss formed a huge lake almost half a mile wide known as the King's Pool or the Fishpond of the Foss. This artificial lake acted as a natural defence and was formed in 1068 by damming the river near the castle. In the seventeenth century it started filling up forming marshy islands — hence the name — but did not finally disappear until the Foss Navigation Company canalised the river in 1792.

The lake was appropriated as a royal fishing preserve which was espe-cially useful when church rules caused fish to be an important item of diet. The King's Fishpool was put in the custody of officers specially appointed by the king who carried out their duties under the direction of the High Sheriff. One such keeper was also gaoler and gate-keeper of the castle. In 1221 ten bream from *vivario de Fosse* were presented as a gift to the Archbishop of York by the Sheriff on a mandate of the king. But in 1293 a Thomas Warthill was sent to gaol for poaching in the King's Fish Pond. The only people allowed to have a boat on the water in 1314 were the Carmelite Monks and that was only to enable them to bring building material across from the Walmgate side. His Majesty also claimed a circuit of land round the pool and this was determined to be "as much as the keeper can mow of the grass and rushes, one of his feet being in a boat and the other foot without upon the ground of the bank".

To ensure the waters were unpolluted Henry IV had passed an order in 1407 that "no dung, excrement or other nastiness to be thrown in the pool. A fine of 100 shillings being payable". But in the eighteenth century due to silting and neglect it had become "the disgrace of York, being in summer time little better than a stinking morass". In 1854 York Corporation bought the fishery rights and immediately started to drain the land, shortly afterwards constructing Foss Islands Road, which you are now following.

Soon you come to the Red Tower, doubtless so called because of the contrast between the colour of its bricks and the sparkling whiteness of the limestone walls, the termination of which it now marks. Built at the edge of an impassable swamp which extended to Layerthorpe Postern in 1490 as part of the defences ordered by King Henry VII, the work was entrusted to bricklayers or tilers. Stonemasons resented this, smashed their tools and threatened to maim or kill them. As a result, when a tiler called John Patrik was found murdered in 1491, the cathedral master William Hyndeley and his assistant Christopher Horner were committed for trial but no conviction was secured.

The tower suffered severely in the siege of 1644 and since then has undergone many restorations due to the nature of the ground on which the foundations are laid. In the eighteenth century gunpowder was manufactured here and it was then known as Brimstone House, whilst a writer of 1855 says "the building is at present used as a pigsty" and it appears to have also served as a stable and cow house. At the side is a projecting lavatory supported on corbels.

As you proceed forward you are rejoined by the River Foss on your left at a small wharf behind which is Leethams Mill. Proudest industrial building of the city and one of its major monuments, Leetham's Mill was built in 1895/6 to designs of W G. Penty. The battlements and cylindrical turret may be concessions to city history but the range of windows, tall recesses, hoists and sheer scale are dramatic on their own. Now renamed Rowntree Wharf, it is intended to house a chocolate experience museum illustrating the history of chocolate production and displaying confectionery crafts for which the city is famous.

Dominating the skyline to your right is the 174 ft high chimney which for nearly 90 years served York's rubbish incinerator but is now a 'retired' architectural feature with the brickwork still showing camouflage paint from the war years. Built in 1898, it has thirteen steel bands around its girth which were added progressively to counteract bulging caused by the ten ton weight of the eight-sided cast-iron mounting which tops it.

Just past it you will see some offices clinging to the face of which is the model black cat symbol of architect Tom Adams. Only a few yards now separate you from Layerthorpe Bridge.

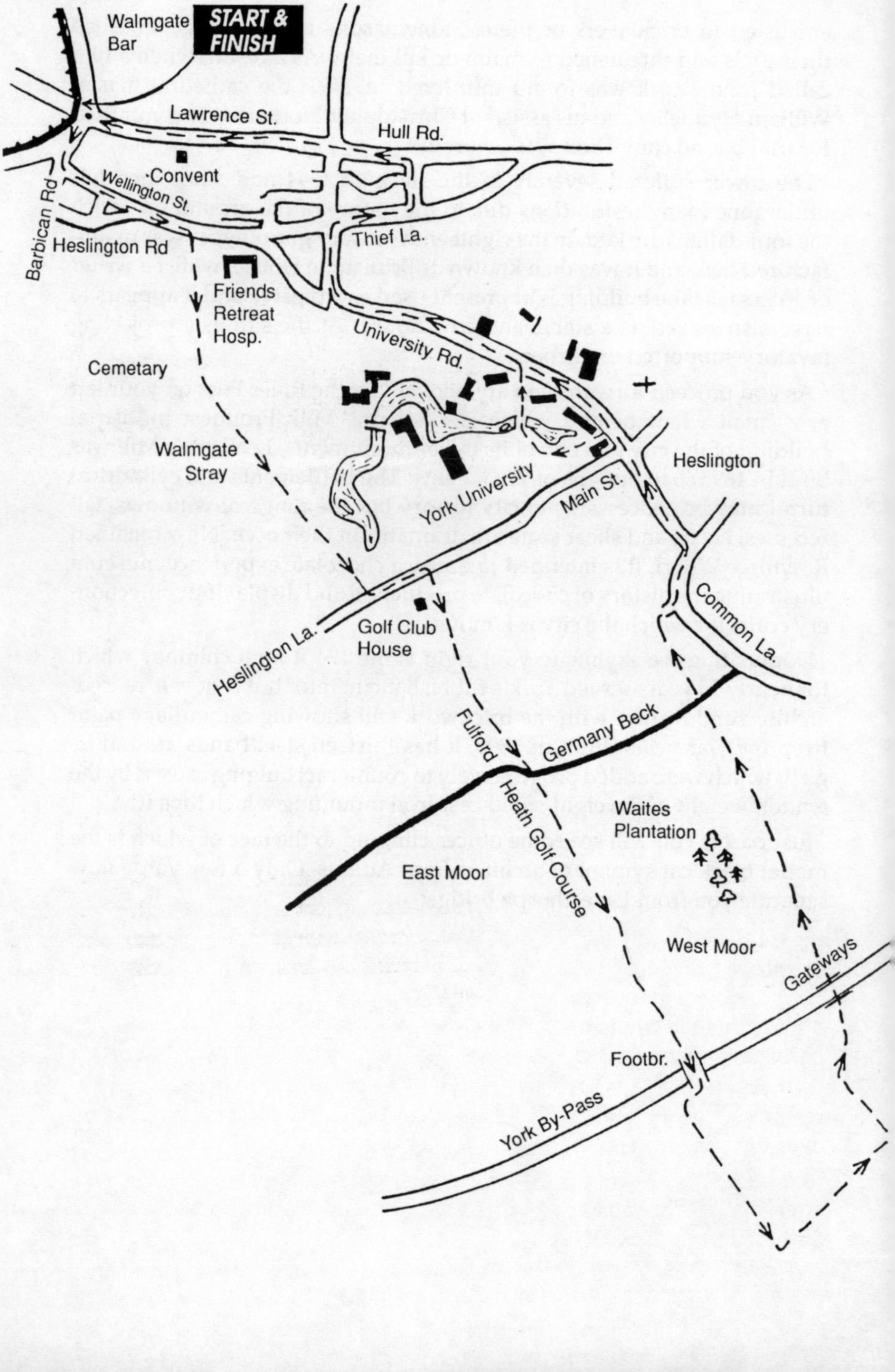

Walmgate
Bar

**START &
FINISH**

Lawrence St.

Hull Rd.

·Convent

Wellington St.

Barbican Rd

Heslington Rd

Thief La.

Friends
Retreat
Hosp.

University Rd.

Cemetary

Walmgate
Stray

Heslington

York University

Main St.

Heslington La.

Golf Club
House

Common La.

Fulford

Germany Beck

Heath Golf Course

Waites
Plantation

East Moor

West Moor

Gateways

Footbr.

York By-Pass

4
Learning from the Wilderness
WALMGATE BAR

Walmgate Bar — Barbican Road — Heslington Road —
Walmgate Stray — West Moor — Tilmire — Fulford Heath —
Common Lane — Heslington Main Street — University Road —
Thief Lane — Garrow Hill — Hull Road — Lawrence Street —
Walmgate Bar.

approx. 7 miles

THE INCORPORATION of a twelfth century archway in Walmgate Bar is evidence that there existed here a stone gateway, through earth ramparts crowned with a palisade, for nearly two centuries before the adjoining walls were built. Here too is retained the barbican as well as the portcullis and fifteenth century inner wooden gates. Yet it has suffered more damage and as a result been more restored than the other gateways. In 1489 it was burned by rebels under John Chambers and battered by cannon stationed on Lamel Hill and in St Lawrence's Churchyard during the siege of 1644.

During the siege an abortive attempt was made to mine it and the visible sag in the side walls of the barbican is probably due to a this. A company of "perdues", as they were called at that time — the equivalent of our modern commandos — had sallied out from the city and captured a soldier of the besieging army, who "being strictly examined by the Lieutenant-Colonel in Clifford's Tower confessed that they were mining, and that they had mined to the middle of Walmgate Bar, and shewed where they had begun to mine, being at a little house on the north side of the said gate; which Sir Thomas Glemham, that gallant and vigilant governor prevented by mining above them and pouring water in upon them". However the structure must have been weakened because it would appear that the whole upper story on the outer side as well as much of the barbican had to be rebuilt after the 1644 siege, completion four years later being commemorated by an inscription over the outermost arch. Further restoration in 1840 is recorded on a tablet below the medieval royal arms over the main outer arch.

Walmgate Bar has witnessed some exciting incidents. King Edward IV after a period of conflict with the Lancastrian forces under the direction of the Earl of Warwick — the 'King Maker' — was compelled in 1469 to flee to Burgundy. He returned with a small army the following year and, landing at Ravenser near Spurn Point, marched on York. After a parley with the civic authorities at Walmgate Bar in which Edward declared that he merely came to claim his personal inheritance: "this noble city is in all our names; you, the Lord Mayor, aldermen, sheriffs, and citizens of York, and I, by my right, the Duke of York, that is all the favour that I desire, that you and I may have the same place invested in our name, which is YORK", he and his force were admitted. There followed the battles of Barnet and Tewkesbury after which Edward was undisputed King of England.

Of particular interest is the inner facade of the Bar for it is a timber-framed and plastered house in the classical style of the late sixteenth century. Still preserved are the Roman, Doric and Ionic columns and mullioned windows. Embellishments recorded in the Chamberlains' Accounts of 1584/6 — such as royal arms and lions in wood or plaster and iron wind vanes — have long since disappeared. Born here in 1793 was John Browne, artist and historian of York Minster.

With the Bar behind you walk a few yards to your right along Barbican Road beside the walls where the rampart was cut back in October 1827 for the pens of a busy cattle market which now exists outside the city at Murton. A charter for the market was granted by Queen Elizabeth I in 1590 although it had been in operation prior to that date and it was held every alternate Thursday between Palm Sunday and Christmas Day. In addition there were three special winter cattle fairs, which were held on All Souls' Day, Martinmas Day, and Candlemas Day every year.

To your left is the bus depot and Spotted Cow Hotel on the site of the mysterious Ace House traced back by Angelo Raine as far as 1575. One suggestion is that it was connected with the preparation of potash for use by York dyers.

Cross the road at the lights to enter Wellington Street and bear left a few yards up Heslington Road towards the large and impressive building called Fairfax House, on your right, which was once the nurses' home for the adjacent hospital and is now university student accommodation. Just past is what was once the tiny Herdsman's Cottage (Number 103) and beside which is the gateway leading into Walmgate Stray, known to local inhabitants as "Low Moor".

A board at the side tells you :

Walmgate Stray consists of about 105 acres of land formerly part of a huge area of ancient pasture land which extended from the suburbs of the walled city of York; from half-year lands outside Walmgate Bar, through Fulford Open Fields, over

Fulford Moor and as far south as the Tilmire.
This large and ancient Stray was intercommoned (i.e.shared by
mutual agreement) *for half-year and full-year pasturing by*
Freemen of Walmgate Ward in the City of York together with
various land owners and commoners from adjacent townships
and villages.
In 1757 an Inclosure Act was passed entitled 'An Act for
dividing and inclosing certain fields, meadows and commons
in the Manor of Fulford in the County of York'. In 1759 the
Inclosure Award was published and, within this Award, an
allotment of about 80 acres of land, known as Low Moor, was
made to the Mayor and Commonalty of the City of York (York
Corporation) to be held in trust forever for the exclusive use
and benefit of Freemen residing in the Walmgate Ward of the
City of York. This allotment of land was awarded to
compensate the Walmgate Freemen for losing their shared
rights of common stray and average over the now inclosed
larger ancient Stray. After the extinction of half-year rights over
grounds in the City suburbs outside Walmgate Bar by an
Inclosure Act of 1824 a further allotment of land was made for
the use of Walmgate Freemen but, since this land did not lie
contiguous to Low Moor the allotted land was sold and the
proceeds expended in 1826 on about 25 acres of land
adjacent to Low Moor, thus forming a single Stray of 105 acres.

Originally, Walmgate Stray was managed for the sole benefit of the
Walmgate Ward Freemen by a working group of Wardens and Pasture
Masters. This system of management continued until 1948 when, by an
Agreement between York Corporation and the Wardens and Pasture
Masters of Walmgate Stray, it was decided that henceforth the Freemen
would surrender their ancient rights of pasturage and that York Corporation would assume responsibility for management of the Stray,
undertaking to maintain the Walmgate Stray as an open space for the
recreation of the public at all time.

Go through two gates and walk forward until you have a panoramic
view of the area from the top of the hill. In 1644, during the great siege of
York, about three thousand troops under the command of Lord Fairfax
and his son Sir Thomas Fairfax were encamped in this area and their
forward battery of cannon did much damage to the city walls, to Clifford's
Tower and to many houses in the vicinity. Sir Thomas, later to be appointed Commander in Chief of the Parliamentary Army, together with
Cromwell, played a major role in the decisive Battle of Marston Moor after
which the besieged city of York surrendered to the Parliamentary Army

on 4 July 1644.

Set amidst extensive grounds on your left is the Friends' Retreat which was founded by William Tuke (1732-1822) who was a leading Quaker of his day. He was helped by his son Henry and by grammarian Lindley Murray. Inspiration for the project was provided when Tuke discovered a Quaker patient being ill-treated in an asylum. Twelve acres of land were bought in 1793 for £1,357. Opened in June 1796 for the treatment of the insane, the Retreat was the first asylum where humane methods were adopted. Here too is a Quaker burial ground.

Proceed down the hill, where cattle and horses graze peacefully in the silence of the open vistas which unfold before you. Pass all the allotments on your right and keep to the right as the path takes you over a little footbridge. Away to your left are the curious roof-top shapes of the University buildings which surround the lake with its jet of water shooting into the air.

Two gates have to be negotiated before you reach Heslington Lane at the city boundary where you turn left towards a well established line of Lombardy Poplars on the opposite side of the road. Immediately past the entrance to Fulford Golf Club is a signposted footpath which runs between trees for a few yards before it becomes a surfaced track alongside the golf course with its clumps of trees and open aspect. The dark red brick buildings across the field to your left are student accommodation and it is a development which won an award for the architects because of the way it blended into the environment.

Soon you cross Germany Beck where, if you are very lucky and very quiet, you may see a heron with its head tucked down waiting to catch fish. This stately grey and white bird with drooping black crest and long yellow bill can sometimes be observed flying over in a sedate, methodical manner with its large wings flapping slowly and legs stretching out beyond the tail giving a stork-like appearance.

Trees give way to open fields on your left, and in the Autumn the ground is carpeted with shades of gold from fallen leaves. Continue forward, keeping to the path, as you climb a slope with a pylon on your left and the golf course immediately on your right until you reach a footbridge over the outer bypass.

Cross and go down the slope before turning sharp right between the timber fencing to continue down another slope. At the bottom turn sharp right again with a white fence on your left bordering the golf course. Go through the copse and just before a footbridge turn sharp left at the public footpath sign with a ditch on your right. Follow the green path around the perimeter of the golf course with a hawthorn hedge screening the fields beyond the ditch on your right and after a while a large bank of hips and haws, gorse, balsam, daisies, scrub and heather.

The shrubby species of hawthorn is often called May as this is the month when masses of fragrant white flowers appear on the thorny twigs. The fruits, haws, are an important food supply especially for the winter visiting thrushes, redwing and fieldfare. The seeds are also collected and eaten by wood mice.

Soon you are confronted by a wide gate and the path turns sharp left at the public footpath sign. Over the gate is Tilmire Common. This is a medieval pasture which has never known the plough and, as a result, is a rich habitat for plants, fungi and birds — owls often quarter the tract in the late evening.

The little owl (*Athene noctua*) is named after Pallas Athene, Greek patron goddess of Athens as well as of wisdom and the pursuit of science. The Romans believed owls were monsters and no self-respecting emperor from Augustus to Caesar himself could be murdered or simply die without first being visited by an owl.

Little is known of the process of reclamation in the Middle Ages and of the arrangement of common fields and meadows. Much of the southern half of Fulford was waste or moor, stretching all the way to Tilmire. There is mention of seven and a half acres in a reclamation there called the "new ridding" when citizens of York were entitled to common pasturage in Tilmire, a right which they maintained after a dispute with St Leonard's hospital in 1401 and which was included in an agreement made with St Mary's Abbey in 1842. The moor also included a turbary (a right to take turf) granted in 1375 by the Abbey. The unlicensed digging of turfs was presented in the Abbey's manorial court in 1447 as well as fishing and fowling in Tilmire, which was described as the Abbey's demesne fishery. The agreement between York and St Mary's in 1484 also confirmed citizen's rights of pasturage in part of the open fields and meadows of Gate Fulford.

Go directly ahead along a well defined track around the perimeter of the golf course with a profusion of heather and gorse between clumps of silver birch. Spread out on your right is the open expanse of Tilmire.

When your reach a derelict building turn sharp left along a track with the golf course still on your left. Ignore a cross track and keep forward until you come to a bridleway gate beside the outer bypass. Cross again to pass through another gate on the opposite side of the bypass and keep going forward along a wide track. Continue forward, ignoring tracks going off to the left, past gorse bushes on your right. Yellow hammer, magpies, and the occasional wren amongst others may be spotted in this ideal habitat for bird life as you proceed up the bridleway before turning right at the playing field to reach Common Lane at Lowfield House.

Turn left up the lane for a short distance before going left again across a small green in front of The Elms bungalows with their pretty gardens to enter Heslington village. The late seventeenth century style buildings on the left bear a plaque which tells you that "These almshouses were erected by Robert, Lord Deramore in memory of his beloved wife Lucy 1903".

Heslington village has some fine examples of seventeenth and eighteenth century architecture as it was the centre of a purely rural community until the coming of the University in 1962 (which accounts for the presence of four banks in the village street!).

The Deramore Arms inn sports the insignia of that worthy family, and Main Street also boasts Laburnum Cottage with a Chinese Chippendale porch. Trees down one side and wide grass verges give a spacious touch to what remains a real 'estate village'

Notice the 'blacked-out' window on the second storey gable end of Bridge Farm on your left. This is a reminder of the days when a rapacious Exchequer levied tax on such 'luxuries'. First imposed in 1695 for the purpose of defraying the expenses and making up the deficiency arising from chipped and defaced coins in the re-coinage of silver during the reign of King William III, the iniquitous window tax lasted for over 150 years. All houses inhabited, save those not paying Church or Poor rates, were assessed at two shillings a year. An added tax was laid according to the number of windows — on from ten to nineteen windows the additional tax was four shillings. Because of the grading of the tax it was possible to qualify for a lower duty by blocking up one or more windows, sometimes even going to the extent of camouflaging them with painted replicas. Responding to critics who claimed it was a duty on "fresh air, light and sunshine", Charles Wood, first Viscount Halifax, undoubtedly earned perpetual gratitude when as Chancellor of the Exchequer he re-

Charles XII inn sign.

Heslington Hall and gardens.

pealed the tax on 24 July 1851.

Almost opposite is the intriguingly-named Charles XII inn. The sign which hangs outside identifies the link with a locally-owned racehorse of that name which won the St Leger in 1839. The race was a dead heat between *Charles XII* and a horse named *Euclid*. It was the first dead heat in the history of the race, and later the same afternoon there was a run-off between the two horses which *Charles XII* won by a head. He went on to win the Gold Cup two days later and was them sold for three thousand guineas. He was destroyed in 1859. To add spice to the story *Charles XII* was walked from York to Doncaster for the St Leger.

At the road junction cross forward with St Paul's church on your right, on a site thought to have served as a church since Saxon times. Built in 1857/8 to designs of J.B. and W. Atkinson, it is early-fourteenth century in style with a broach spire.

To the North is Lamel Hill where

Sundial on Heslington Hall.

Fairfax positioned his cannon to bombard the city during the siege of 1644. Historian Francis Drake records that "several batteries were erected against the city, particularly on a hill near Walmgate Bar, where four pieces of cannon played almost incessantly on the tower, castle, and town.

On your left is the administrative headquarters of the University housed in the beautiful Elizabethan hall. Heslington Hall, previously the home of Lord Deramore, was built between 1565 and 1568 for Thomas Eynns, Secretary of the Council of the North and to accommodate Queen Elizabeth when she visited the north, but she never used it. In 1601 it was sold to the Hesketh family and managed to survive the great siege before passing to the Yarburgh family in 1708 when its gardens were formally laid out. It was rebuilt or extensively recast to designs by P.C. Hardwick between 1852 and 1855. Some of the more extreme elements of Hardwick's design were removed by alterations of 1876 and 1903. A Henry Moore sculpture and some marvellous trimmed yews — like rows of discarded hats — behind fountains in a formal pond enliven the gardens.

As long ago as 1641 and 1648 the City of York petitioned the Government to establish a university but the requests were not granted until 1962. Now covering 185 acres once owned by the Deramore family, the University preserves ancient yew hedges and an exquisite summer house in a land-scaped setting around an artificial lake which is quite a wildlife reserve. Boards placed at intervals around the lake illustrate the varieties of water fowl that can be found there. Overlooking it is the strangely shaped

Cog wheel sculpture outside Goodricke College.

Central Hall which is the venue for many kinds of concert from pop to classical music.

On the lawn outside Goodricke College is a giant cog-wheel sculpture representing the star-system Algol which was among the discoveries of John Goodricke. Eldest child of Henry Goodricke of York, he was born at Groningen in the Netherlands on 17 September 1764 and died, unmarried, at York on 20 April 1786. In his short life he "earned lasting distinction by his investigations of variable stars" for which he received the Copley medal in 1783 and at the age of twenty-one became the youngest ever member of the Royal Society.

Water fowl on the University lake.

If you have time you can walk around the grounds by entering through a small archway on your left immediately after the bus stop and exit by crossing the footbridge over the lake near Central Hall and walking through to the main road. Otherwise climb the gentle slope of University Road for a birds-eye view of the campus on your left.

To your right is Heslington Hill and the tumulus of Siwards How. Dominating it is the water tower of York Waterworks, built in 1955 with a million-gallon capacity and believed to be the largest in Britain.

Born towards the end of the tenth century, Siward was a giant in stature, of Herculean strength, and of great courage, which he displayed on many a field of battle.

University Central Hall and lake.

He murdered his uncle to become Earl of Northumbria and in 1041 put down an uprising at Worcester against a new tax with great barbarity, slaughtering, plundering, and burning the city with the blessing of Aelfric, Archbishop of York.

In 1054 he was sent by King Eadwarde in command of an expedition into Scotland against the usurper Macbeth, in favour of the young Prince, Malcolm Canmore, son of the murdered King Duncan — an incident immortalised in Shakespeare's tragedy *Macbeth*.

Siward was eighth of the rulers to live at York and although all had been born fighters, he was the greatest of them all. Stricken with dysentery and rapidly growing worse he lay in his vice-regal mansion without hope of recovery.

When he felt his last moments approaching he suddenly started up from his couch and exclaimed:

"Let me not die the death of a cow! If it be not my fate to die gloriously on the field of battle, as my brave boy, Osbert, has done, with all his wounds in front, at least let me die in the guise of a warrior. Don me my harness, place the helmet on my head, and gird my sword on my thigh. It were a shame and disgrace that I, who have faced death on so many fields, should die ignominiously in bed. Bring forth my battle-axe and shield, and place them by my side, that the ghosts of my warlike ancestry who are looking down upon me now, may see me pass away from earth to join them in their everlasting home, with the semblance of the great warrior that I have been." (As recorded by Frederick Ross in Yorkshire Family Romance.)

And so, seated in a chair, clothed in his armour and supported in an upright posture by his attendants he died, as he had lived, in war-harness. He was buried in St Olave's church.

Continue forward to the junction and turn right into Thief Lane which tells its own story. Take the first turn on your left Garrow Hill Avenue — next to Siward Street — and drop down to Hull Road.

Turn left along Hull Road and on your right will see the Beeswing public house with its sign which clearly demonstrates that it has no affinity with the winged insect but commemorates a famous northern racehorse — winner of thousands of pounds in more than fifty races nearly 150 years ago. Today the legend lives on with the Beeswing Stakes at Newcastle.

Beeswing pub sign.

Beeswing, as a two-year-old, won the Champagne Stakes at Doncaster and followed in 1836 with wins in the St Leger Stakes and Gold Cup at Newcastle. The mare was prevented by one second place in 1840 from winning the Gold Cup at Newcastle every year from 1836 to 1842. Four times the sprinter took the Queen's Plate and Her Majesty's Plate at the August meeting at York. At the age of nine in 1842 she also won the Ascot Gold Cup.

Notice the colourful stained glass

butterflies in the ground floor windows of the pub. Hereabouts once stood the church of St Nicholas which in 1428 had an annual value of £5. A considerable amount of skirmishing took place around here during the siege of 1644, doubtless occasioned by attempts on the part of the royalists who held the city to silence Fairfax's cannon on Lamel Hill. During the course of this, according to one historian, the church "was quite ruined" and not rebuilt. Three bells from the church were given to St John's, Micklegate in 1653 and its Norman porch was re-erected at St Margaret's, Walmgate in 1684.

Soon you will come to Milton Street and Nicholas Street on your right which commemorates St Nicholas' Hospital designed for lepers and almost certainly the first to be established for this purpose in York. An enquiry of 1275 found that "Matilda, the good Queen of England" gave to the master and brethren one carucate of land (i.e. as much land as a team of oxen could plough in a season) and one and a half acres of meadow in the suburbs of York, with the distinct stipulation that the brethren for ever should find victuals for all lepers who should come there on the even of the Feast of St Peter and St Paul — that is 28 June. These lands were in the locality of Layerthorpe and Tang Hall. However the hospital is said to have been founded by King Stephen in 1141 and a Royal Visitation held in 1303 to inquire into its administration indicates that it could accommodate forty residents. If the inmates fared as well as the lepers who came to the hospital on 28 June they did very well, for Queen Matilda also stipulated that they should receive "bread, ale, a mulvel with butter and salmon when in season, and cheese".

Early in its history the hospital seems to have suffered from mismanagement. In 1285 an inquisition was held by the then Mayor, John Sampson and Thomas de Normanvill, concerning "the affairs of the hospital of lepers of St Nicholas, York" and in 1292 it was "found to be in a state of decay, by reason of the inept and inordinate conversation and administration of the masters and brethren and sisters against the statutes and rule". In that year articles were drawn up by the Archdeacon of York for the management of the hospital, which were ordered to be read annually before the brethren and sisters in their church. But in spite of this ordinance there are many subsequent records of misrule. The siege of 1644 appears to have completed its ruination.

On your left as you continue forward is the Convent of Poor Clares. The York community of this sisterhood dates from 1865 but they did not enter this permanent residence until 1872.

Only a few yards now separate you from Walmgate Bar.

5
Matters Matrimonial and Military
FISHERGATE POSTERN

Fishergate Postern — Tower Street — Brownie Dyke —
New Walk — Fulford Ings — Selby Road —
Fulford Road — Cemetery Road — Melbourne Street —
Fishergate — Fawcett Street — Fishergate Bar —
Paragon Street — Fishergate Postern.

approx. 3½ miles

BUILT ABOUT 1505 to replace an earlier structure called Talkan Tower after Robert de Talkan, Mayor in 1399, Fishergate Postern Tower for some unknown reason was in the seventeenth century called Edward's Tower. The three-storeyed tower has surprisingly few military features and the first floor has a projecting lavatory which at one time issued into the waters of the lake below — for the King's Pool once flowed right up to the base of the tower, separating it from the castle.

From the Postern, walk alongside the walls to your left to reach a pedestrian crossing over the busy Fishergate — 'the Street of the Fishermen' — recorded from about 1080. Now turn right to return past the ornate front of Number 16 on your left which is the century-old family decorating

Masons Arms. Glass inn sign.

firm started by Thomas Metcalfe Oxtoby when he was a teenager and now run by the third generation. Continue forward to pass The Mason's Arms pub built in 1935 on the site of an older one, using internally a splendid Gothic oak fireplace of 1830 and panelling from the court room on the first floor of the old gate-house of the castle. Notice the unusual glass sign, and on the left hand stone corbel at the entrance is a colourful example of the city arms whilst the right hand corbel boasts the Yorkshire rose.

Ahead is Castle Mills bridge

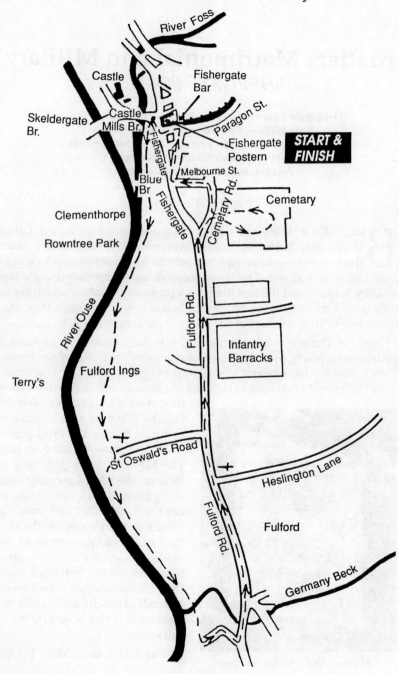

which carries Tower Street over the River Foss. In 1583 it was agreed that a wooden bridge for "footmen and horsemen" should be built here but this was destroyed in the siege of 1644. In 1733 this was ordered to be replaced by an arch horse-bridge, only for this to be washed away in 1746. In 1793 a high arch bridge was built which was rebuilt and widened in 1800 by the Foss Navigation Company, with further improvements being carried out by the Corporation in 1836/7 before a new and substantially wider bridge was built in 1955/6. Alongside the river on your right is Raindale Mill and the eighteenth century wall of York castle; this was one of the castles built by William I in 1068/9 on the natural defensive site provided by the confluence of the Rivers Ouse and Foss.

Turn left through the iron gate to go down the steps alongside the Lock House which carries a wooden board lettered "Brownie Dyke".

On your right is Castle Mills Lock built in 1794. Under an Act of 1793 the Foss Navigation Company had been given 'power and authority to purchase Lands, Tenements and Hereditaments . . . and to make and maintain a navigable communication for Boats, Barges and other Vessels . . . from the Junction of the River Foss with the River Ouse . . . to Stillington Mill.'

And if newspaper reports are to be believed, it was in this river that the first recorded iron craft was launched. The *York Courant* of 27 May 1777 reports: "Last Tuesday a new Pleasure-Boat, constructed of sheet iron was launched into the River

Castle Mills lock and barge.

Foss. She is 12 feet in length, 6 in breadth, has sailed with 15 persons in her, and may be conveyed to and from the river by two men".

On your left is the rear of the £1.1 million Novotel and a modern housing development which stands on the site of the Anglo-Saxon city of Eoforwic — once the bustling hub of York's trade and industry. Officially opened on 14 May 1988 it boasts 124 bedrooms, a free in-house TV channel, conference and banqueting centre, swimming pool and restaurant.

On this site too in the thirteenth century stood St Andrew's Priory. In 1292 a royal licence was given to the prior to enclose a lane from Fishergate to "the water of Use" but the canons seem to have been less fortunate than other orders in obtaining revenues and the priory fell on hard times. In 1538 it was surrendered to the King and in 1546 granted to John Bellew and John Broxholme following which everything seems to have been demolished since there was no mention of any buildings in the Act of 1547.

Here in 1794 John Prince set up a glassworks and also acted as travelling salesman for its products, but when he died in 1820 so did the business. It was revived in 1835 with the establishment of the York Flint and Glass Company by Joseph Spence and friends who produced decorative bottles bearing coats of arms, bee-hive glasses, drawer nobs in crystal, sapphire, jet, or canary yellow topaz. Despite these exotic creations the firm foundered in 1921. Nine years later the National Glass Company restarted the business which was modernised and successful enough to become a public company in October 1948 with four directors, one of whom was Sir Ivo Thomson. Once again it foundered and was closed in December 1983 with the site being cleared to make way for the present development.

The River Foss with a catchment area of 125 square kilometres discharges into the River Ouse where the lower reaches originally formed a moat augmenting the formal defences along the eastern boundary of the city. A £4 million flood alleviation scheme here was officially opened on 28 February 1989 by John MacGregor, Minister of Agriculture, to protect nearly 600 homes affected by serious flooding in 1982. The scheme includes an 8 metres wide by 7½ metres high steel turnover lift gate weighing 16-tonnes, which is closed when the Ouse rises 2.8 metres above normal level, and a pumping station with eight pumps that discharge flood water from the Foss downstream at a rate of 1,800 tonnes a minute

Walk forward to the confluence of the two rivers at Blue Bridge which derives its name from always being painted blue. A plan of 1736 shows a bridge here built after the corporation ordered "Wardens of Walmgate to get such bridge as they thought proper made over Browney Dyke (the Foss as far as the lock) at the New Walk in St George's Close". The Corporation paid £110.7s.0d for this simple wooden drawbridge which was replaced in 1768 by a stone bridge with a wooden swivel section in the centre to allow the passage of masted vessels. The present structure is the sixth on the site. The concrete emplacements on either side were meant to hold two cannons taken from the Great Redan at Sebastapol during the Crimean War, but in 1941 they were sold for scrap to help the war effort.

To your left is Blue Bridge Lane. This formed the southern boundary of the grounds of St Andrew's Priory founded in 1202 for monks of the Order of St Gilbert of Sempringham. Although the grounds covered about six acres the monastery never figured much in city life and when it was "axed" in 1539 there was only a prior and three monks.

Continue forward through the stile in the railings alongside a wide gate. Sparkling ladies of Georgian York and their attendant beaux had high social ambitions so in 1731 a forward-looking Corporation hit on the idea of a promenade alongside the Ouse. Two years later, trees were planted and a broad, gravelled walk was laid out on the riverside. William Etty R.A., famous nineteenth century painter and son of York claimed "no public walk in Europe is superior, if equal, to it". New Walk, as it came to be called, has since been widened, extended and had more trees planted along it to become a spacious promenade offering varied views of the Ouse and craft plying on it.

River Foss flood barrier.

Well House by John Carr.

Near the southern end was a spring of water called 'Pikeing Lady' or 'Spring Well' which in the eighteenth century was believed to have medicinal powers. As a result, in 1756 the Corporation arranged for a well house to be built around it by famous architect John Carr. The York Chamberlain's account book of 16 May 1757 records: "Paid to Mr John Carr for erecting the building about Pikeing Well, he having allowed £25 for his freedom, £63.13s".

Continue past the Well House and alongside a red brick wall to the end of some mature trees to pass through a gateway and a line of new trees on the right. Continue forward across the green sward alongside the river bank where on the morning of Sunday 11 June 1797 two officers in the 46th Regiment of Foot stationed at York fought a duel. The cause of the quarrel between Mr George Crigan, surgeon to the Regiment, and Lieutenant-Colonel Bryan Bell, is unknown but we do know that the surgeon was killed and the colonel, with his two seconds, was arrested and imprisoned in York Castle.

Evidence given to the jury at the subsequent murder trial must have persuaded them this was an affair of honour and that some justification existed for the challenge. Suffice it to say the murder charge was reduced to one of manslaughter and the officer escaped the trip to the "three-legged mare of York". Instead he was sentenced to a month in the city gaol on Ouse Bridge and fined six shillings and eightpence (33p).

Such a minor punishment clearly insulted the defunct surgeon whose ghost shows his displeasure over the vagaries of English law by "stalking about" the scene of his demise.

Where access along the bank is obstructed by a fence, cross diagonally to your left to a gravel path which leads to St Oswald's Church dating from about 1150, which was replaced by a new church in 1866 and not used this century. The parish registers show that during the 1730s and '40s there was a large number of marriages conducted in the church with neither bride nor groom coming from Fulford. More curious is the very strange entry in the parish register of 26 May 1744 which reads: "Samuel Mason buried who was married seven years and found out to be a woman at his death.

In 1973 the church became redundant and in 1981 following restoration was converted into a private dwelling called St Oswald's Hall, which is open to the public. Its furnishings create an authentic interior of a small fifteenth century manor house and art treasures include icons, illuminated manuscripts, medieval wood-carving, metalwork, embroidery, and a good collection of early oak furniture. In the grounds a small enclosed garden contains species of plants recorded as having been grown in the medieval period.

Archaeological excavations have revealed traces of Prehistoric, Roman, and Saxon occupation and foundations of two earlier buildings on the site. Victims of the Black Death were buried here in 1349.

Associated with the former burial ground is the ghost of Holy Trinity Church, Micklegate. Legend has it that a wealthy householder who died and was buried at Holy Trinity, left a widow and child who regularly visited his grave in company with the family nurse. The child fell victim to the plague and in accordance with a Corporation ruling was buried at St Oswald's. Mother and nurse visited this grave too until the mother died after which the ghost came weekly to receive the child's ghost from the grave and together with the ghost of the nurse went to the grave at Holy Trinity to coincide with the time of service there — to the consternation of the congregation. As a local poet put it:

> *Now hand in hand -*
> *Like airy things they've past,*
> *With noiseless step, and with burdened smile,*
> *And meek eyes heavenward last:*
> *Like things too pure upon earth to stay,*
> *They have fled like a vision of light away.*

Cross St Oswalds Road and go forward along a wide track which skirts York Motor Yacht Club founded in 1934 and boasting moorings for about thirty craft. Spare a thought for poor William Johnson of Naburn who, on 27 October 1447, was fined fourpence because he trampled and depastured the lord's herbage on the banks of the river by dragging his boat through.

The path makes a sharp right turn towards a green hut on the river bank which marks Fulford Moorings before crossing Fulford Ings, scene on Wednesday 20 September 1066 of the Battle of Fulford where Earl Tostig, bent on recovering his lost earldom and supported by the forces of Harald

St Oswald's Hall, Fulford.

Hardrada, King of Norway, clashed with the men of Jorvik led by Morcar, Earl of Northumbria and his brother Edwin, Earl of Mercia.

The most reliable account of what followed is in the Icelandic saga of Snorri Sturlsson written after 1220. He tells us:

> *"Harald (Hardrada) began to array his men. One wing stood upon the river bank and the other higher up, near a ditch which was deep and broad and full of water. The Jarl's (Jorvik) men let their arrays go down along the river and most of their men. The standard of Harald was near the river; there the ranks were thick, but they were thinnest at the ditch, and least to be depended upon.*

Thither Morcar came down with his standard. The wing of the Northmen by the ditch retreated, and the English followed them, thinking they were going to flee, but when Harald saw his men retreating along the ditch, he ordered a war-blast to be blown and urged them on. He had the standard 'Landwaster' carried forward, and made so hard an attack that all were driven back. There was great slaughter in the Jarl's host.

Morcar's brother had his standard brought along the river, downward against the army of Harald, but when the King hardened the attack, the Jarl and his men fled along the river upward. Only those who followed him escaped, but so many had fallen that large streams of blood in many places flowed over the plain.

When the Jarl had fled, Harald surrounded Morcar and the men who had advanced along the ditch with him. The English fell by hundreds. Many jumped into the ditch, and the plain lay so thick that the Norsemen walked across it with dry feet on human bodies. There Morcar perished."

The Norwegians won and ravished York but only five days later, on 25 September, retribution followed with a resounding defeat at the Battle of Stamford Bridge. The survivors could man only twenty-four of the 315 ships that had brought the invading army up the River Ouse to Riccall.

Oh Fulford the peaceful; what telling shall show us
The blood that was shed on they borders of green?
Till York made surrender to Harold Harfager,
And bowed were the gates of the Northern Queen".

Across the river is the great bulk of Terry's chocolate factory and the banks hereabouts boast a profusion of willow herb, vetch, balsam, thistles and other wild plants.

Until 1828 there were two Fulfords — Water and Gate — but in that year they were united into Fulfords Ambo, meaning 'both Fulfords'. This is one of several names used over the years and doubtless is derived from the foul or muddy ford over the little stream called Germany Beck which feeds into the river. More noble, but less credible, is the suggestion that the name might be associated with Fulloaydes, Duke of Britain, who, as commander of the Sixth Legion, tried to beat off a Pictish attack on Eboracum in AD364.

With all the skills that local novelists have shown, it is surprising that nobody has worked out a romance set in the ochre-coloured walls of Water Fulford Hall, for both its situation and architectural features would seem to invite such an effort. The jutting porch and oriel windows lend character to its riverside location on your left, whilst the unobtrusive and secretive appearance in its tree-clad frame could add charm to any well-worked story.

If further attractions are needed, what could be better than an eighteenth-century square dovecote which, we are assured, by A.G. Cooke in his *Book of Dovecotes*, is a good example of its type. The sides are 20 feet long, and it is 18 feet high to the slope of the roof, with a cupola and about 570 L-shaped nests arranged in fourteen tiers. When a rope is pulled inside the cote, the holes in the cupola are opened to liberate the pigeons.

Towards the close of the sixteenth century the house was the home of an old Lincolnshire family called Key, one of whom served as High Sheriff of that county. In this capacity he was frequently called on to settle disputes as to the ownership of swans by Fenland farmers who kept large numbers of these royal birds. In an effort to avoid conflicts and simplify the decision when one arose, he invented a system of marking the bill of each bird in accordance with a master chart he devised. This long, narrow, parchment scroll, bearing the drawings of a number of swans' bills all differently

Dovecote at Fulford.

marked, with details of ownership — a kind of private heraldry — was still in his possession when he moved to Water Fulford Hall.

Soon you cross a stile beside a slipway and then Germany Beck as the river swings westwards. This strange name is thought to originate from the time when a certain German de Brettgate had a toft and croft in Fulford (1258-1270) where the main road crosses the beck.

About 1616 a bold plan was put forward to build a gigantic tidal canal of about 25 miles in almost direct line from Germany Beck to Blacktoft on the Humber. As always, finance was scarce, and York Corporation sought support from James I when he visited the city. Arriving at Ouse Bridge, the King was welcomed by a brief charade composed by a local rhymester.

This was produced "to declare the shallowness of the River of Owse", and in one memorable line the tired river, who was the chief speaker, declares: "I scarce have means to ebbe or power of flowe". The plea seems to have touched the royal sympathies, for James encouraged the Corporation to persevere and promote the necessary Act of Parliament. Tenacious almost to the point of desperation, they persisted, but their efforts never came to fruition for one reason or another.

After crossing another stile the path now joins a wide tree-lined track which turns left to a gate. Here a notice from Fulford Parish Council tells anyone about to enter that "Land beyond this point has been registered as a village green. Therefore no vehicles are allowed access under the Inclosure Act 1857 S.12". Follow the winding lane to reach Fulford Road — A19 York to Selby — where you turn left opposite a green recreation area.

The first house on your right — Number 151 — apart from a garden with herons and other ornaments has fixed to it, beneath a keystone dated 1905, a plaque which reads:

> To the memory of the officers, non-commissioned officers and men of the East Yorkshire Regt who lost their lives in the service of the country during the South African War, 1900, 1901, 1902.

After listing the dead the inscription concludes:

> This cottage was erected by comrades and friends of the regiment in the East Riding of Yorks. and the site presented with a donation of £200 by Capt. Key of Fulford Hall in memory of his son Lieut J.P. Key, East Yorkshire Regt., who died of wounds received at Thabanchu, Orange River Colony 3rd April 1901.

Proceed up Fulford Road, bordered by properties which reflect the character of the old village — numerous cottages with hanging baskets of flowers in Summer and pyracantha adding a dash of colour to their walls. The Bay Horse Inn on the right is soon followed by the Plough Inn on the left and are reminders of the agricultural heritage of the village.

York Pavilion, on your right, now a hotel and restaurant, is a fine Georgian house which was once the home of musician John Barry who composed the themes for all the James Bond films. Previously called Fulford House, it was acquired by William Richardson in 1751 and formerly belonged to a member of the Redman family. It was enlarged in the late eighteenth century after 1845 when a different William Richardson bought the adjoining property to extend the site.

Dick Turpin House on the left has a novel metal sign to remind us that in W Harrison Ainsworth's romantic novel *Rookwood — Dick Turpin's Ride to York* the hero came this way. Turpin, with pursuers hot on his heels, had been obliged to swim Black Bess across the River Ouse at Cawood. Ainsworth tells us:

> *'Once more, on wings of swiftness, she bore him away from his pursuers, one of whom observed "it is but an expiring flash; that gallant steed must soon drop".*
> *Contrary to all expectations, however, Bess held on, and set pursuit at defiance . . .*
> *Fulford is past. The towers and pinnacles of York burst upon him in all the freshness, the beauty, and the glory of a bright, clear, autumnal morn..".*
> *"It is done — it is won", cried Dick'.*

Almost opposite is the Saddle Inn with its old gas lamp converted to electricity, and close by a small cottage which once served another purpose as the inscribed stone over the door testifies: "This SCHOOL was Founded & Endowed by JOHN KEY ESQ in 1771". Next door are houses with tall finials which are a reminder that it was once considered prudent to include these to deter witches from resting on the roof-tops. A few yards more, and on the left, you reach the White House, a stuccoed two-storey building with iron balconies to its first floor windows. The Old House on the left is Georgian, and the Old Vicarage on the right has an unusual frontage taken up entirely by two bay windows.

The 140 foot high spire on your right is Fulford Parish Church of St Oswald designed by Pritchett & Son. The site was bought in 1864 for £450 and the corner foundation stone laid on 23 May 1865 by Captain William Henry Key of Water Fulford Hall. Opened on 24 December 1868, it was destroyed and restored to the same design after a fire in 1877.

Set around a green square on the left are the Hunt Memorial Homes by Needham Thorpe and White built in 1954.

On your left is the Gimcrack Hotel which keeps alive memories of a famous racehorse. The Ancient Fraternitie of Ye Grimcracks, the oldest racing club in the world, was formed in York in 1770 in honour of the gamest of racehorses, *Gimcrack*. Although winning twenty-seven of its thirty-five races, ironically *Gimcrack* never won at York but its pluckiness was considered well worth commemorating. That game little horse is still remembered each year by the Gimcrack dinner and the Gimcrack Stakes. The Gimcrack Stakes was first run in 1846 and was won by Ellendale, owned by Admiral Harcourt. This splendid mare also won the Richmond Cup in 1848 and this was presented to the York Race Committee in 1924 by Admiral Harcourt's great-nephew, the Hon Gilbert Johnstone, and it is exhibited each year at the Gimcrack dinner.

In front of a garage on your left near Maple Grove is the stump of Fulford

Cross which for many years marked the boundary of the city's jurisdiction. Records of 1374 and 1445 describe the cross as being made of wood but the present stone remnant is believed to have been one of the crosses erected when the pestilence of 1604 afflicted York. Here country folk could offer their produce for sale without entering the city.

In August 1541 King Henry VIII and Catherine Howard made a Royal Progress through the northern counties and came to York to stay for twelve days and receive the submission of those who had been implicated in a recent rebellion. The royal party approached the city through Fulford instead of the customary route through Tadcaster. The King was met at Fulford Cross by the mayor, aldermen, and others, who received

Fulford Cross.

him on their knees, whilst a humble address was read by the recorder.

The unusually large entrance doors and size of the garage is a reminder of its original purpose — as a tram depot. On Saturday 16 November 1935 the last electric tram in York made its farewell journey from Nessgate to Fulford depot, driven by the Lord Mayor W.H. Shaw under the guidance of an inspector J.A. Stewart who had driven York's first electric tram in 1910.

The Tramways Brass Band led a procession into the depot around midnight where a 'funeral service' was held and a trumpeter sounded the

Last Post as the epitaph was given.

Ashes to Ashes, dust to dust
The Corporation won't have us
The West Yorkshire must

On the opposite side of the road are Imphal Barracks originally built for the infantry in 1874 and next to them the site of the former Cavalry Barracks.

By the middle of 1877 York Infantry Barracks had opened to house the officers and men of the 14th Regimental District on one side of the square and the West Yorkshire Regt (14th Foot) on the other. Today, Inphal Barracks — so named in 1951 to commemorate exploits in Burma — is the Headquarters North East District and Headquarters 2nd Infantry Division.

Preserved here is a colourful crest with an inscribed plaque which reads:

This Coade crest shows the arms adopted by George I on his accession to the throne in 1714 and which continued in use until 1801.
The quartered arms represent England impaling Scotland, France, Ireland and Hanover.
The relief moulded example was executed by Charles Coade in 1796 using his reconstituted stone.
It was part of the pediment of the Cavalry Barracks Officer's Mess which was removed in 1971 and then renovated and erected in 1978

The astonishingly imperishable artificial stone was invented by Coade in the latter half of the eighteenth century and the secret of its composition died with his widow.

Also preserved here is a 25 pounder gun and a Saladin armoured car. For security reasons the barracks are not open for public inspection.

Before 1792 the country had no official barracks for troops. Parliament saw the army as "agents of the Ministers of the Crown", and were not prepared to see them housed at the country's expense. William Pitt, in 1792, fearing a war on the Continent and anxious to have a reliable fighting force at his disposal, launched into an ambitious barrack-building programme — without the necessary Parliamentary approval.

Three years later York Cavalry Barracks, one of the oldest in the country, was built under the guidance of Lieut Gen DeLancey, the man appointed by Pitt as his Barrack Master General.

Three troops of Sir Watkin William Winn's Ancient British Fencibles were

The Coade crest.

the first soldiers to be stationed there.

The two architects, James Johnson and John Sanders, appointed for ten shillings a day and two and a half percent commission on all building work, were directly responsible to the Barrack Master and both he and his department became the subject of a military enquiry in 1805.

Questioning revealed that the Commander-in-Chief's instructions to build, and the Secretary of War's sanction to finance, had been verbal in nearly every case.

In the years between 1792 and 1804, during which time the York barracks were finished, the Barracks office had designed 141 buildings! Most of them, it seems, were carried through by word of mouth.

An independent valuation of the work showed some discrepancies with the builders' accounts sufficient to suggest negligence on the part of the architects and surveyors — in this case, two and the same: Johnson and Sanders. The inquiry condemned the department for not settling accounts quickly, for not having accounts audited and not keeping a closer check on the quantity and quality of materials used.

The whole barrack department was heavily censured especially when embezzlement was detected in another department.

York Cavalry Barracks came in for its share of criticism: "Cavalry Barracks present some remarkable errors in construction and internal arrangement. In the great majority there are no litter sheds and horse litter is piled on the pavement against the walls directly under the men's windows, which are generally placed over the stables . . .".

Another discomfort and indignity hardly likely to endear the army to potential recruits was the urinal tub; a large wooden barrel set in the centre of the barracks and used by the soldiers at night.

The army tried to combat this by issuing each man with his own chamber pot before finally building what they called "night urinals" adjoining the sleeping quarters.

The Cavalry Barracks, last occupied by a horse regiment before the First World War, said farewell to the horse at the outbreak of the Second World War when the 15/19th Hussars switched to armoured cars. Now the site is the Divisional Headquarters of North Yorkshire Police.

Opposite is the now vacant site on which formerly stood the military hospital and where was held the first show of the Yorkshire Agricultural Society. Formed on 29 August 1837, the society decided to hold a show "for the general improvement of agriculture, more especially by the exhibition of breeding stock and Agricultural implements". This was held on 29 August 1838 and attracted nearly 5,000 visitors.

Cross the road at the zebra crossing to Fishergate Post Office and bear right along Cemetery Road alongside the railings between pillars crowned with a sarcophagus, sphinx and an urn at the handsome gates from the Walker Foundry. Pass through these gates.

The cemetery came into being in 1836, being provided by a private company after the Corporation had refused to take any action to meet what was then becoming an urgent necessity due to traditional city burial grounds being incapable of expansion. A public meeting on 1 July resolved to form a cemetery beyond the walls for persons of all religious denominations and capital was raised by issuing shares valued at £10 each.

Some eight acres of land situated a mile from the Bars at Micklegate, Bootham, Monkgate and Layerthorpe Bridge, a quarter mile from Walmgate Bar and Ouse Bridge and half a mile from Foss Bridge, was duly acquired. The grounds were laid out by one of the shareholders, the architect James Pigott Pritchett, who was a favourite among Nonconformist chapel builders.

On an elevated terrace is the chapel, the first stone of which was laid on 4 April 1837 by the Lord Mayor, James Meek. Capable of holding three hundred people, the chapel is built of white stone from Roche Abbey and is modelled on the Temple of Erechtheus at Athens. Consecrated on 14 September 1837 it is now listed by the Department of the Environment and is amongst the eight percent most important listed buildings in the country.

By June 1848 some 2746 burials had taken place and the cemetery was taking over half the city's dead. The consecrated land was extended to the east following purchase of a field from Samuel Tuke (of the Retreat) and this brought the area to eleven acres, estimated to be enough to cope for a century.

The cemetery became the last refuge of citizens of every social order from prominent people such as Lord de Grey, Joshua Terry, and Lord Mayors like George Leeman, to the poorest in the community, including Richard Chicken — the likely prototype of Dickens' Mr Micawber, who died in the workhouse. Sculptors John Atkinson and William Plows, antiquarians William Hargrove and Harvey Brook and engraver Henry Cave are buried here as well as members of the Terry families.

Despite the early optimism as to capacity, major extensions had to be made in 1872, 1924, 1931 and 1941, bringing the total to about 30 acres, and by the early nineteen-fifties there was no more space available so the company was eventually wound up in 1966. There are about 121,000 graves, with fine examples of carved Victorian memorials beloved by our forefathers in a landscaped setting which is worthy of detailed exploration.

Frank Buck's gravestone car.

Immediately inside the gate is the modern marble headstone, hand-carved in Italy, to Frank Buck which would not be remarkable except for one thing — on top is carved a very accurate replica of an Austin A95 car. Clearly discernible is the registration number FB600 — a cherished number including the owner's initials. Frank Buck was a scrap dealer and vintage car enthusiast who also had a 1915 Ford.

In contrast in the south western corner is a neo-Jacobean obelisk commemorating the Leetham family who owe the present form of their name to a barely literate eighteenth century vicar of Acaster Malbis where they farmed. They brought grain up the River Ouse and became millers in the 1860s. A prosperous business enabled them to live in style at Beech House on The Mount, Elm Bank, Tadcaster Road, and Aldersyde, Dringhouses. Towering above the River Foss since 1896 is their mill which is one of the city's major industrial monuments, but the business failed in the 1920s.

Recalling that a vast chicory business flourished in and around York during the mid-nineteenth century is a cross to William Wilkinson Wilberforce. Growers sent their crop to merchants who prepared it for sale as an additive to coffee. One such merchant was Henry Wilberforce of Walmgate who died in 1876 but whose son William carried on the business and also became Lord Mayor in 1880. During his year of office the York Tramways Company opened a horse tram system with his active support — rewarded by a directorship.

Among the 250 military heroes buried in the cemetery is Thomas Wilkinson — one of the first men to win the nation's most prized bravery award, the Victoria Cross.

Born in Marygate in 1831, Thomas joined the army on 23 November 1850, serving with the Royal Marine Artillery from HMS *Britannia* at Sebastapol where he was specially commended for his brave conduct on 5 June 1855. He risked his life over a long period as he carried sandbags in exposed areas to rebuild gun emplacements. For this he received the Victoria Cross. On retiring from the Army in 1859 he returned to York, later becoming manager of a sand yard and he died on 22 September 1887 after a long and severe illness, aged 55.

Leave the cemetery by the same gate you entered and turn right before crossing Cemetery Road to the Melbourne Inn and bearing left into Melbourne Street past lozenge-shaped Victorian front gardens. Number 24 has a model cat sat on an upstairs window ledge and some houses have keystones with floral and foliage decorations picked out in different colours. On the corner where you join Fishergate, with its two gilt clock faces on each corner, is Tower House — the block of army offices built in 1878 when the headquarters of the north-eastern military district was transferred from Manchester to York.

Turn right and keep to your right up Fawcett Street. On your left are The Woolpack and The Shire Horse pubs with the York City Arms Sports Club boasting a colourful city crest on the right.

This street is part of the original Fishergate of the Middle Ages which continued through Fishergate Bar and included the straight portion of the present George Street on the right of which is St George's church. In the cemetery opposite, there is the grave of Dick Turpin. The inscription reads: "Richard Palmer, alias Richard Turpin notorious highwayman and horse stealer executed at Tyburn, April 7th 1739".

Fishergate Bar is one of the ancient "side doors" through the city walls which existed from the fourteenth century and was sometimes known as St George's Bar but the present gateway dates from the fifteenth century. Above the wide central arch with its scorched grooves is an inscription from 1487 when the Lord Mayor, Sir William Todd constructed 60 yards of wall at his own expense.

In 1489 Parliament authorised a tax on land to finance war against Brittany. Payment was resisted and an appeal to King Henry VII was rejected and the Earl of Northumberland was despatched to instruct the nobility and gentry to meet him at York and pay up. Rioting ensued in which the Earl and some of his servants were slain whilst a number of buildings around Fishergate Bar were destroyed by fire — and hence the scorch marks on the stone today.

Fishergate Bar.

The rioting developed into open rebellion under the leadership of Sir John Egremond and "a fellow of mean degree" called John a Chambre. The rebellion was quickly suppressed. Sir John Egremond escaped to Flanders but John a Chambre was captured and hanged at York, on a gibbet of unusual height specially erected on Clifford's Tower whilst a number of his followers were hanged upon a lower staging around him.

Fishergate Bar was walled up and remained so for the next 340 years until a new cattle market outside the walls was built in 1827. Under Elizabeth I and her successor it served as a prison for Roman Catholics and lunatics.

Turn left along Paragon Street for the few yards alongside the walls which terminate at Fishergate Postern.

On Hallowed Ground

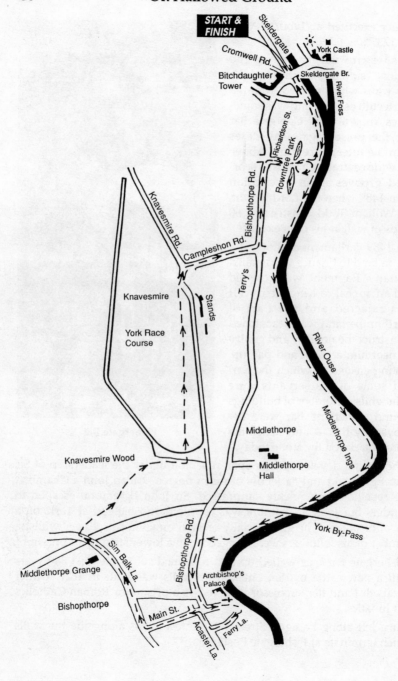

6

On Hallowed Ground
SKELDERGATE POSTERN

Skeldergate Postern — Terry Avenue — Nun Ings —
Middlethorpe Ings — Bishopthorpe Road — Chantry Lane —
Ferry Lane — Bishopthorpe Main Street — Sim Balk Lane —
Green Lane — Knavesmire — Campleshon Road —
Bishopthorpe Road — Richardson Street — Rowntree Park —
Terry Avenue — Skeldergate Postern.

approx. 4½ miles

THE CORPORATION discussed Skeldergate Bridge over the River Ouse for only five years before beginning to construct it. And on 1 January 1881, only 2½ years after the foundation-stone was laid, it was opened for pedestrian use and formally opened for general traffic on 10 March 1881. But by then it had cost £56,000 — more than half as much again as the original estimate. The little castellated toll house is a reminder that for thirty-three years, until 1 April 1914, it cost a halfpenny to cross.

On that date a civic procession in full dress paraded from the Mansion House to the toll-booth for a ceremonial "re-opening" at which the Lord Mayor paid the last toll before "the Corporation party proceeded across the bridge to confirm its freedom, as it were". The enthusiastic crowd who watched may have been less good-humoured when they found their rates bill had been increased by three farthings in the pound for the next twenty years to meet the shortfall resulting from the abolition of the tolls.

As Ald. Sir Joseph Sykes Rymer, grand old man of the council — he was Lord Mayor in 1887, 1899, 1907 and 1912 — pointed out: "It is always a confounded nuisance to have to put your hand in your pocket and take out a half-penny for a toll, but I don't know that people are any fonder of paying rates".

It was designed by Thomas Page — also responsible for Lendal Bridge — but he died before the council approved his plans and the job was taken over by George Gordon Page. Unlike Lendal Bridge the new bridge had to cope with tall-masted ships and was designed in three sections, a land arch over Skeldergate itself, a main arch over part of the river, and a small arch which was moveable to allow navigation. By 1971 the lifting mechanism had seized up and a new fixed surface was laid over it.

In the river wall of the Bonding Warehouse alongside are fragments of a building known as Hyngbrig Tower which marked the end of the walls, and where they crossed the street was a gate called Skeldergate Postern. This archway, flanked by two turrets, was taken down in 1808, provoking a lawsuit between the Archbishop and the Corporation who lost and were deterred from further demolition.

Now the walls end at Bitch-daughter Tower in the shadow of Baile Hill which is the principal remaining feature of a castle built by William the Conqueror. It passed into the custody of the archbishops of York about 1200, together with a large area of adjoining land which the *Domesday Book* calls 'The Archbishop's Shire'. Later it was used for grazing cattle, for musters of armed citizens, archery practice, trials by wager of battle, and for traditional Shrove Tuesday games. In 1802/7 the City and Ainsty Gaol was built here but demolished in 1880 when some of its stone was used to build Skeldergate Bridge. Consequently today's Cromwell Road was formerly Jail Lane.

Bitchdaughter Tower.

The demand for a bonded warehouse was first heard around September 1833 when a meeting of merchants and tradesmen met to discuss the idea, but the project was abandoned. Thirty-eight years were to elapse before the Corporation made up its mind to provide one "as early as practicable". They chose a site which had been the centre of the city's river commerce in the Middle Ages, next to the Old Crane Wharf, and on 26 May 1873 the bonded warehouse was opened for business. Charges, including bonding-rent and storage, were: "every butt, pipe or puncheon 2s. 9d a week, hogshead 1s7½d, quarter cask 1s 1d, case of one dozen bottles 2¼d, between one and three dozen 4½d, over three dozen 7d". The warehouse was quickly filled to overflowing, having become "more crowded than is consistent with convenience and safety", as William Ryley of the Inland Revenue Office put it in a letter to the Town Clerk. Next year an adjoining building of three storeys and about double the floor space

The Bonding Warehouse.

was happily built for £168 11s 6d less than the £2,175 estimate.

Evidence of the thriving river-borne commerce which was carried on here in the fifteenth century is to be found in the city accounts where charges are recorded for the use of the Old Crane Wharf. Wine, spices, grain, salt, wax, steel, iron, linens, lead, sea-coal, woad and madder — names which seem strange to our ears nowadays — were all handled here.

This trade may well have been the origin of the name, although Skeldergate is said by some people to owe its existence to being the home of shield-makers. However others claim it is derived from an old dialect word 'upskill', meaning 'to unload' as when tipping a cart, and this seems more likely.

Either way it was chosen as a location by Wilkie Collins, novelist friend of Charles Dickens, for his book *No Name*; and Robinson Crusoe was born there in 1632 according to author Daniel Defoe.

With Skeldergate behind you, go under the bridge to enter Terry Avenue and follow the river bank. On your right is a multi-million pound development of 134 flats and luxury penthouses called Bishops Wharf, begun in 1988, which stands on the site of the former Henry Richardson & Co fertiliser works whose wharf was adjacent. In their sales literature at the turn of the century they were recommending early orders of guano, assuring customers "we supply ourselves with this article by sailing vessel, week by week, according to the demand — the very small profit on Guano not allowing of railway carriage — and as 'wind and wave' are proverbially uncertain, we sometimes have to wait a few days for the arrival of vessels".

Just before you reach the first turning on your right — Clementhorpe — there stood until the late 1920s a boatyard whose slipway into the river had to be crossed by a wooden footbridge. Complete with timber stores, sawpit, blacksmith shop, paint and tar shop, office and so on, it was used to build barges for commercial operations. The Slip Inn further up the street perpetuates its memory. This was probably also the boathouse for *Royal Carolina* — the Lord Mayor's state barge launched on Thursday 28 June 1733 and named after the Consort of George I. The vessel, which had a sumptuously decorated saloon and an elaborately carved bow or figure-head, was rowed by a crew of twelve. Eight years later, on 27 December 1741 after the River Ouse had been frozen for twenty-two days, melting ice floes sunk the vessel.

Keep forward and a little further ahead on your left are offices in a building which once served a different purpose for the York Cooperative Society. Set in the brickwork at the corner is a stone inscribed :

BAKERY. THESE PREMISES WERE OPENED ON 14th JANUARY 1903 BY COUNC. W.H. SHAW DIRECTOR.

Bishops Wharf across the River Ouse.

The whole area on your right is known as Clementhorpe which some authorities claim means "a small village colonised from a larger one" and this could allude to its location outside the city walls or the foundation of a breakaway religious house.

As you follow the river you pass the very attractive gates that mark the entrance to a park. Two plaques mounted in an archway beside a little lake tell its story. They read:

This park and the adjoining playing fields were given to the city by Rowntree & Co Ltd at the close of the Great War (1914-18) as a tribute to the memory of those members of the company's staff who at the cost of life or limb or health and in the face of indescribable suffering and hardship served their country in her hour of need. Many were inspired by the faith that this war might be the end of war — that victory would lead to an enduring peace and to greater happiness for the peoples of the world. The creation of a League of Nations would be a fitting crown to the faith and hope of the men who have fought and a true memorial to their endurance, heroism, comradeship and sacrifice.

That hope was not to be fulfilled and the second plaque reads:

The gates at the entrance to this park were given to the City of York by Rowntree & Co Ltd in memory of all those from the Cocoa Works who lost their lives in the Second World War (1939-45) and in thanksgiving for the courage and steadfastness of the people of York throughout those years.

Except the Lord keep the city;
The watchman waketh but in vain.

The gates are believed to be the work of the French smith, Jean Tijou, probably the best craftsman of all time in this particular field, and it is understood that he made these gates in 1715 for Richmond Park near to Windsor Great Park. The leaf and beadwork shows the high standard of craftsmanship of that period. On either side of the gates the curved wings, consisting of wrought iron railings, which are lower than the main gates, have small statues carved in Portland stone and give scale and importance to the central gates.

Tijou was a Frenchman who had been compelled to leave his country together with many of his Protestant fellow craftsmen following the revocation of the Edict of Nantes in 1685. After some years in Holland he came to England in 1689 and William III became one of his patrons resulting in screens and gates at Hampton Court Palace.

Beyond the park the road swings sharply to the right up Butcher Terrace but you should keep to the river bank to follow a grassy track which enables you to inspect the back gardens of property fronting Bishopthorpe Road. The river makes a wide sweep here and there is an old tradition that any person throwing five white pebbles into the Ouse as the hour of one is struck on the first morning in May will then see everything he or she desires to know, past, present and to come, revealed on the surface of the water.

In pursuit of this belief many people tried the charm, amongst them a knight returning from the wars, who wanted to know how things faired with his lady-love. He came to the riverside and threw in the pebbles at the proper time, but to his dismay he beheld the home of the maiden to whom he was engaged where a youth in mask and cloak was descending from her window, whilst a servant was hiding the ladder on which the ascent had been made.

Maddened by jealousy at the sight of his lover's frailty, he jumped on his horse and hastened to Scarborough where his girlfriend lived. He rode all night, and as dawn broke, his horse dropped dead in sight of the mansion, so he continued on foot. There, as foretold, was a youth ascending a ladder. He rushed forward and stabbed the ascending form to death, only to discover it was his betrothed who had been to a dance in fancy dress and, returning late, was intent on getting into the house without awakening her parents. The head-strong knight lived with the anguish and remorse for his rashness many years afterwards for his thoughtless action which had sacrificed the life of his true-love.

You next cross Nun Ings and to your right is the detached clock tower of Terry's which overlooks the five storeys of mullioned and transomed windows beneath an enormous crowning cornice of the neo-classical factory building designed by J.G Davis and L.C. Wade in 1925/30.

Terrys of York originated in 1767, dealing in candied peel and general confectionery. In the 1820s the partners, Messrs Bayldon and Berry, were joined at their premises near Bootham Bar by Joseph Terry, a Pocklington farmer's son who trained as an apothecary dealing in medicines in Walmgate. In 1824 the business moved to larger premises in St Helen's Square and by 1840 Joseph Terry was in sole charge selling products in seventy-five towns and cities in England.

These products included candied citron, mint cake, coltsfoot rock, acidulated drops, cough mixtures, lozenges, and Pontefract cakes.

He died in 1850 and his son, who later became Sir Joseph Terry, took over the business.

In 1862 further growth resulted in a move to a factory downstream from Skeldergate Bridge at Clementhorpe, which took deliveries of raw materials — sugar, cocoa, glucose, orange and lemon rind, and coal — twice weekly by steam boats.

Chocolate manufacture began in 1886 before the move to the present "factory in a garden". Here it needed to enclose a river-water header-tank, treatment equipment and a chimney. The result was the 134 feet 6 inches high red-brick tower with four clock faces each eight feet in diameter. Instead of numerals the clock has ✷ T E R R Y ✷ Y O ✷ R K on the faces.

Terry's, which has a workforce of about 2,000, lost its independence to Forte's in 1963, became part of Colgate-Palmolive in 1977, and was acquired by United Biscuits in 1982.

Famous brands include *All Gold, Moonlight, Chocolate Orange*, and *Pyramint*.

The river makes a wide sweep around Middlethorpe Ings as you follow the path over three stiles. Clusters of ramsons or wild garlic scent the air between April and June and the bright pinky purple tubular flowers of the foxglove appear on tall stems between June and September. Also known as Dead Man's Fingers, all parts of this tall plant are poisonous but medicinally the drug digitalin is used to treat heart conditions. The insides of the flowers are paler and have a heavy pattern of spots to guide bees and other insects up to where the nectar is.

Here, so it is said, on dark nights appears a headless lady clothed in white, sometimes waiting underneath a particular tree. Apparently during the eighteenth century a woman living alone near Bishopthorpe was believed to be very wealthy and one autumn night some unknown intruder after her valuables murdered her. The corpse was hidden in long grass under a clump of trees.

Weeks passed before the body was discovered and as a result of decomposition by that time the head had become separated from the rest of her body. She was buried in the churchyard of St Andrew at Bishopthorpe, but ever since at the witching hour she leaves the grave to wander the tree-lined towpath in pursuit of her murderer.

The once lonely river banks are now held in the grip of the twin concrete viaducts carrying the York outer bypass. The £750,000 five-span bridge was opened on 14 April 1976. Go under and cross another stile to be rewarded with glimpses through the trees of Bishopthorpe Palace, home of the Archbishop of York.

The title Archbishop has been held since AD735 when Egbert, cousin of King Coelwulf received the official appointment from Rome.

After yet another stile the path narrows with trees on either side with great clumps of Indian balsam flourishing in the marshy undergrowth. The path turns sharp right around the perimeter of the palace grounds to a gate on to Bishopthorpe Road where you turn left.

On your right is the parish church of St Andrew built in fifteenth-century style between 1888-1903 by Hodgson Fowler. In the churchyard is a memorial to Walter Brierley, said to have been one of the best architects to have practised in York.

In the north aisle is the Kate Ruth Kirk memorial window which was given in 1953 by her husband Cecil George Kirk. The upper panel depicts the holding of the Manor Court after the conveyancing of the estate from the Abbot of Kirkstall near Leeds to Walter de Grey. Also shown is the Archbishop repealing the severe Game Laws in 1226. The lower panel shows King Charles I at Bishopthorpe in 1633 performing "The ceremonies for healing them that be diseased with the King's Evil" (scrofula).

National history too is enshrined in a stained glass window given in 1951 in memory of Harrison Woodward's family. One panel shows Archbishop Drummond's church from 1765 to 1842 and the other shows it after Archbishop Harcourt had refaced the west end in stone in 1842. The bottom panel shows a dramatic scene of a tragic event in our history; Archbishop Scrope, manacled, with two other nobles, also manacled, being condemned to death in the presence of King Henry IV.

Another window worthy of notice was given by Kate Ruth Kirk in memory of her sister Jessie Oliver who was headmistress of St Thomas' Church of England School, Stepney from 1897 to 1945.

An educational theme based on Bishopthorpe was chosen with one panel showing school life in 1693 on the assumption that there was a school here since Thomas Early in his will of that year gave £2 to be paid annually out of his estate at Bishopthorpe, to a schoolmaster.

Church and school links are shown in a second panel as a reminder that in 1846 Archbishop Harcourt built a school here; the headmaster is depicted teaching vulgar fractions and on the blackboard is the problem $\frac{3}{4} \times \frac{5}{6} =$. The answer is not given but is left to the observer. A third panel shows teacher and scholars in 1950, with the old classroom clock by W Storey of Tadcaster (1846) showing 26 minutes to 11 — almost break time.

Preserved here also is a thirteenth-century piscina from the old village church; a fifteenth century font, said to have come from a destroyed church in York; a table about four hundred years old; and statues of St Peter and St Andrew each side of the east window. An inscription perpetuates the memory of Archbishop William Thompson who died here in 1890.

Kate Ruth Kirk Memorial window.

There is a nice human touch about the story of how William Thompson became Archbishop in the nineteenth century. He heard the news while recovering from illness at Oxford.

He rose from his sick bed and went to tell his wife: "My dear, I am the Archbishop of York" to which the good lady replied: "Oh, do go and lie down".

Carved in the oak roof above are the correct armorial shields of seven famous Archbishops of York who have lived at Bishopthorpe Palace and worshipped in the village church — Walter de Grey, Henry Drummond, Markham, Harcourt, Musgrave, Thomson and McLagan.

Skirting on your right the tree-shrouded palace grounds, alive with squirrels and many species of birds, you arrive at the fanciful gatehouse. Adorned with battlements, pinnacles. gargoyles and pyramid canopy, it was built almost entirely of stone from the ruins of Cawood Castle by Archbishop Drummond in the middle of the eighteenth century. The blue-faced six-foot-wide clock in the tower was salvaged from a former stable block and is inscribed 'T.H. 1744' which is believed to refer to Archbishop Herring.

The site was bought in 1226 by Archbishop Walter de Grey for his palace, and the Manor of Thorpe St Andrew took on a new role and a new name. Here in 1405 Archbishop Richard Scrope, described as "learned, charitable, devout, humble-minded, courteous and affable to all" stood trial in the great hall for rebelling against Henry IV, and when Chief Justice Gascoigne refused to pass sentence, the King ordered a local lawyer called Fulthorpe to pronounce judgement.

Many prelates spent much time here but Cardinal Wolsey never entered

Harrison Woodward family window.

Section of the Jessie Oliver window.

the palace during the sixteen years of his archbishopric. In August 1617 King James I "rode in his coach through the city with all his train to Bishopthorpe, where he dined with Archbishop Troy Matthew".

At one time passing sailors would fire a salute and be rewarded by the Archbishop with flagons of ale, but Archbishop Musgrave stopped the custom and thereafter the bargees always seemed to find it necessary to emit quantities of black smoke as they passed Bishopthorpe. Archbishop Greenfield had to issue a licence for officials to sprinkle holy water in St Martin's churchyard after it had been polluted by the nose bleed of a youth fighting there; and the citizens of York came out in 1832 to burn in effigy Archbishop Vernon Harcourt when the House of Lords rejected the Electoral Reform Bill.

Archbishop Sweal de Bovill quarrelled with the Pope over the appointment of an Italian to the deanery of York and was suspended, then excommunicated, and Archbishop Magee, a robust Irishman, who died suddenly after a few months, left behind him the much-quoted remark that he "preferred to see England free, to England sober".

Archbishop Thomas Savage came to Bishopthorpe from Rochester in 1501 and was said to be "a mighty hunter". In the second year of his office, the King's Fishpool of Foss was leased to him and his successors for twenty-one years. In the same year he became President of the King's Council in the North.

Archbishop Lancelot Blackburne (1724-43) was said to have been thrown out of Cambridge for some misdemeanour and ran away taking his tutor's violin with him and playing his way to London with it. He is said at one time to have been a pirate before he became Archbishop when he returned the violin to its owner and at the same time asked him if he would like to be Archdeacon of Holdernesss.

Is this an over-simplification of the facts? A romantic tale that should be taken with a pinch of salt?

Historian C.B. Knight suggests that shortly after Blackburne's ordination he went to the West Indies and served for a time as chaplain on a buccaneering ship which went on a marauding expedition against the Spaniards.

Apparently in 1702 he had found it necessary to resign the sub-deanery

Bishopthorpe Palace gatehouse.

of Exeter because of scandalous reports.

With one of those quick swings of fortune that seem to abound in the past, he was reinstated in 1704 and obtained high preferment.

He became Dean of Exeter in 1705, Bishop of Exeter in 1717 and came to York in 1724. His final promotiom was attributed to the gratitude of King George I for assistance which Blackburne had given him in a questionable matrimonial affair.

George I had imprisoned his wife Sophia Dorothea of Zell in 1682 because of a suspected intrigue, and it was rumoured that the king had been secretly married to the Duchess of Munster by Blackburne.

Resting in York Minster's Lady Chapel "in the hopeful expectation of the last trumpet" is the delightfully named Archbishop Accepted Frewen, who took office in 1660, the year of Charles II's restoration, and died four years later.

At Bishopthorpe Palace in 1662 he rebuilt the great hall in unusual rusticated brickwork, with an elaborate plaster ceiling.

He is said to have been "a bachelor of deepest dye" and would not permit a female servant to be employed in any capacity whatever at the palace.

Walk around the corner of the grounds and turn left down Chantry Lane which takes you back to the river bank past Ramsey House on your right. Named after the previous Archbishop of York, who had just been enthroned as the 100th Archbishop of Canterbury in 1961, the house was built for Mr Arthur Gladwin. He was a Methodist preacher for more than sixty years and a former joint general manager of the Yorkshire Life Assurance Company. He died aged 88 in February 1983.

Past it is an excellent view of the palace back garden and ahead is the ruined old village church of St Andrew's, built of red brick in 1768 by Archbishop Drummond on the site of a much older stone church which dated back to 1215. In 1842 Archbishop Harcourt restored it but the River Ouse gradually eroded the foundations and it was largely pulled down in 1899.

The beautiful west front still stands proudly enriched with leafy niches, pinnacles and buttresses with faces and finials, whilst a bellcote crowns its gable. On the site of the altar Archbishop McLagan put up a tall cross and on this is written: "On this spot there stood for centuries the Parish Church of St Andrew, Bishopthorpe. Rebuilt on another site AD1899". Archbishop Drummond and his two grand-daughters are buried under the cross.

Bank-protection here was an unending burden for the villagers and as long ago as 1619 the church wardens were being reprimanded for neglecting their duties in this respect, whilst a curious fine imposed in 1623 was devoted to the same purpose. In that year Richard Sherburn Esq of Mitton-in-Craven and Ellen Gregson were prosecuted "for suspicion of fornication together". They were found guilty and penance was imposed, afterwards commuted into a fine of £150 to be devoted to pious purposes. Of this sum £20 was expended "in making a Cawsey in the lane at Bishopthorpe, and for the defence of the churchyard there from the River of Owze".

In 1892 the churchyard was almost entirely under water and the site was abandoned in favour of a new one behind the palace.

Bear right a short way along the river bank to reach a bungalow beside Ferry Lane where you turn right. In 1899 the parish council decided that all material being off-loaded at the ferry landing and not intended for use in the village should be charged three pence a ton. Also, if goods remained on the landing for more than a fortnight, five shillings was to be charged. The objective of this substantial penalty was less to raise revenue and more to keep the landing clear for Mr J. Sanderson who was paying one shilling a year for the privilege of using his ferry-boat. This income went to the vicar who owned the ferry rights and had always had more than a passing interest in the river since the establishment of St Andrews Church somewhat too close to the invading waters. Doubtless in the thirteenth century the vicar thought York too close for comfort too, since he was required to have his Sunday dinner each week with the servants of the nuns of Clementhorpe to whom his church was appropriated. "If he complains of the food he must wait until he receives it quietly" ordered the authoritarian nuns.

At the top of Ferry Lane turn right again and then left into the main street of the village, passing on your left the Ebor Inn which was originally The Brown Cow, but nobody seems to know why the name was changed. In 1884 the inn was sold by Tadcaster Tower Brewery as The Ebor and the inventory, which listed eight rooms including a dairy and a brewhouse, also included in the sale iron and wooden spittoons and the form with a stuffed seat.

Continue forward up Main Street and you will see on your right the Cooperative store with a sundial inscribed *Tempus Habile* (Time is Fleeting). A stone lozenge with the initials TPM and the date 1691 no longer exists but it used to be on top of a row of cottages called Sundial Terrace — two of which were demolished to make way for this store before 1909.

A little further along, also on the right, is The Marcia public house. *Marcia*, alias *Spiderbrusher*, was a famous racehorse bred by the late William Fenwick. In 1776 the horse won 125 guineas and a hogshead of claret from Sir Laurence Dundas's *Pontac* at York and went on to win other races at Lincoln and Morpeth. In 1777 she became the property of William Garforth who named her *Marcia* for whom she also won several races before she died in the Spring of 1779.

Almost opposite on the left is The Woodman pub with its colourful tiled sign put up when it was modernised between the wars

Walk forward to the road junction where on your left you will see a small building with clocks on each corner and facing you an inscribed plaque which reads:

This church school and site was given by Edward Vernon Harcourt, Archbishop of York 1846. Commemorative stone replaced by Bishopthorpe Youth Club 1969.

Turn right up Sim Balk Lane and on your right set back immediately past the Spar grocery store is No 34 Bell Cottage which dates from the 1770s and used to be two cottages which were united in the 1970s. There are some bells hanging on the outside but they have nothing to do with its name which came from 'Granny Bell', the village midwife who used to live here. Above the front door is a blocked in window painted to match the other sash windows and designed to avoid the window tax of the nineteenth century.

Continue forward and, after passing over the brow of the bridge which crosses the outer bypass, drop down to a gateway and stile on your right which mark the entrance to a cycleway and pathway formerly called Green Lane.

Follow this around the back of Knavesmire Wood on your left, which was probably planted in 1774 by Thomas Halfpenny, the archbishop's gardener at Bishopthorpe who was one of the founder members of the Ancient Society of York Florists in 1768. He was the father of artist Joseph Halfpenny(1748-1811)

Just before the long straight of the racecourse, join the path beside a gorse bush on your left which leads under the rails and directly across the Knavesmire in front of the main stand. Racing has been held here since 1730 and during the First World War it also served as a base for the Royal Flying Corps until May 1916 when it moved to Copmanthorpe following an attack on the city by a Zeppelin Airship. On 21 February 1913 the first aircraft ever to land in York touched down here piloted by Captain Longcroft. More than six thousand people turned out to greet three machines of the Royal Flying Corps on their way from Farnborough to a new base at Montrose, Scotland. Five aeroplanes had set off but mechanical problems forced one down at Doncaster and another south of Selby.

Inside the main grandstand on the fourth floor is the York Racing Museum and Library; a peaceful sanctuary from the raceday bustle, and an absorbing shrine to the late, the great, and just plain bizarre.

There you can marvel at the 9¼ lb hairball taken from a horse's stomach; an old enema funnel; a pair of castration clamps; and even a pair of leather encased equine spectacles!

Whole cabinets are dedicated to famous horses like *Mill Reef* and *Brigadier Gerard*; various racing plates together with mounted hooves commemorate *St Simon* and *Hyperion*; *Voltigeur*'s leg can be inspected, and there is even a cigar case from the hide of the famous *Eclipse* himself. A lock of hair from *Arkle* and and the racing plate of *Golden Miller* recall famous steeplechasers, whilst numerous pictures, books, racing calendars, famous silks, and paintings salute the 'sport of kings'.

Whips of the racing heroes can be seen, including that used to such good effect in 1985 by Steve Cauthen to carry off four of the five English Classics. And a whole cabinet is dedicated to Fred Archer exhibiting the colours worn by the thirteen-times champion jockey when winning the 1886 Derby on *Ormonde* — arguably the greatest horse of the century. Archer's boots and spurs are also proudly displayed, together with a crimson nightshirt embroidered with the great man's monogram.

When you reach the end of the course at the corner of Knavesmire Road turn right along Campleshon Road which gained its name from a tailor called Thomas Campleshon who was one of the City Chamberlains in 1612. After passing a school, note the second turning on your left which is Kensington Street and only a few yards from the junction with Bishopthorpe Road.

Opposite the junction is Reginald Terrace and Reginald Grove, once the gardens of Sir Ivo Thomson. And the man who earned a few shillings tending them as a jobbing gardener was George Russell, the 'lupin man'.

Born in 1853 at Stillington, ten miles north of the city, he was the fifth son of a master shoemaker. Around 1918, at the age of sixty, Russell began his great love affair with the lupin. Tradition has it that he was looking at a vase of typical dull and short-spiked dark blue lupins in the drawing room of one of his employers — Mrs Micklethwaite of The Mount — and reflecting gloomily how poor they were. Then he conceived the idea of trying to improve on nature.

He set to work on his four allotments between Terry's factory and Bustardthorpe (now a barren race-day car park) on your right. During the next eighteen years he persevered, devoting most of his spare time to breeding new improved strains of hybrid lupins. So the colourful, modern Russell lupin that we know so well today was conceived.

To daily travellers along Bishopthorpe Road he was a familiar sight, with his mass of white hair, bending over the lupins, and always he was working. Even in winter the kitchen of his home at 20 Kensington Street was utilised to prepare for the coming season, for example chipping lupin seed to ensure better germination. Here, as on the allotments, he was assisted by Sonny, son of Mr and Mrs Heard who lived next door at number 22.

Russell obtained seed from all over the world and spent the best part of two arduous decades sowing,selecting and crossing. By the early 1930s the bright dawn of success had blazed across two allotments as they were awash with rainbow hues.

Not surprisingly they were a local scenic wonder and attraction: when Bishopthorpe and South Bank folk took a walk they went with the specific objective of going to see Mr Russell's lupins.

"With a veritable blaze of rich and exotic colour, the Russell Lupin literally burst upon an astonished gardening world on a June day in 1937". So wrote Ronald Parret in the opening words of his small book *The Russell Lupin*.

It was James Baker, a nurseryman from Codsall, who persuaded Russell he ought to share his strains of lupins with the world. The *Gardeners Chronicle* reported:

> On a considerable wall space Messrs Baker have displayed a magnificent collection of the Russell lupins. These lovely varieties represent 20 years work by a little known gardener who has produced strains of surprising excellence which are characterised by dwarf, sturdy habit, and long erect spikes of many lovely colours.

In the next few years Baker sold more than 60,000 plants a year and world-wide sales of seeds exceeded a quarter of a million packets.

In 1937 Russell had been awarded the Veitch Silver Memorial Medal by the Royal Horticultural Society and received the MBE in 1951. But the loyalties of his life are commemorated in the twenty-two named varieties of lupin he created — for example City of York and Sonny. He died in October 1951.

Cross Bishopthorpe Road and turn left before walking forward to Richardson Street on your right. Turn down to enter Rowntree Park which is well worthy of inspection before exiting at the far side to Terry Avenue where you turn left to return along the river bank to Skeldergate.

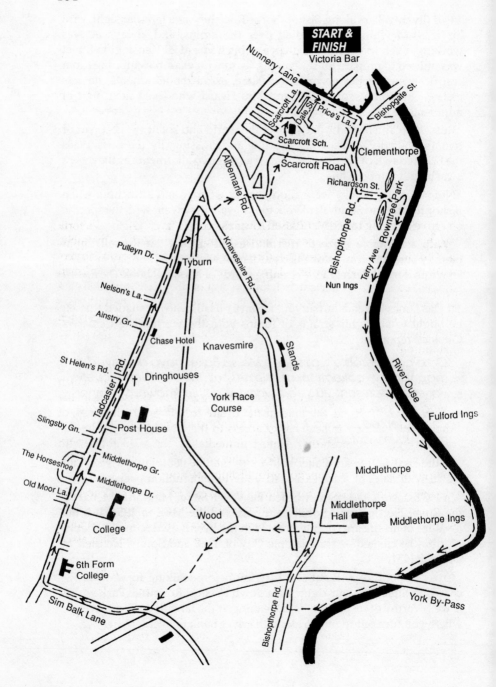

START & FINISH
Victoria Bar

Nunnery Lane

Scarcroft La.
Dale St.
Price's La.
Bishopgate St.

Scarcroft Sch.

Clementhorpe

Scarcroft Road

Richardson St.

Albemarle Rd.

Bishopthorpe Rd.

Rowntree Park

Terry Ave.

Pulleyn Dr.

Tyburn

Knavesmire Rd.

Nelson's La.

Nun Ings

Ainstry Gr.

Chase Hotel

Knavesmire

St Helen's Rd.

Tadcaster Rd.

Dringhouses

Stands

York Race
Course

River Ouse

Fulford Ings

Slingsby Gn.

Post House

The Horseshoe

Middlethorpe Gr.

Old Moor La.

Middlethorpe Dr.

Middlethorpe

College

Wood

Middlethorpe
Hall

Middlethorpe Ings

6th Form
College

Sim Balk Lane

Bishopthorpe Rd.

York By-Pass

7

Tales of the Turf
VICTORIA BAR

Victoria Bar — Nunnery Lane — Prices Lane — Bishopgate Street —
Bishopthorpe Road — Richardson Street — Rowntree Park —
Terry Avenue — Middlethorpe Ings — Bishopthorpe Road —
Green Lane — Sim Balk Lane — Tadcaster Road —
Scarcroft Lane — Victoria Bar.

approx. 6 miles

A S THE INSCRIBED PANEL over the central arch relates, Victoria Bar in Nunnery Lane was pierced through the walls " . . . by Public Subscription under the direction of the City Commissioners AD1838, George Hudson Esq. Lord Mayor". In the process, workmen discovered a blocked ancient arch known as 'Lounlith' or the hidden gate of medieval records. Iron studs above the bar were used as strengtheners to hold the crowds who came to see the Prince and Princess of Wales when they visited York in 1866 for the Yorkshire Fine Art and Industrial Exhibition.

Turn left down Nunnery Lane which takes its name from St Mary's convent founded in 1686. As far back as 1243 it was called Bagergate which in 1303 had become Baggergate and in 1546 Beggergate. This was from the vagrants who utilised the lane in the desire to avoid the challenge of Micklegate Bar and to seek easier access to the city by way of the less carefully guarded posterns. Almost immediately the road forks with Nunnery Lane going right and Price's Lane going left alongside the walls. Follow the walls to the junction with Bishopgate Street.

Facing you is the Swan Inn whose history can be traced back to 1856 when Thomas Staverley, a one-eyed man from Stockton-on-Tees, established a shop and beer-house here, although it was not named at that time. He sold the property in 1861 to pay off a large mortgage and it passed through the hands of several owner-landlords — by 1887 it had become known officially as the Swan Inn — before 1899 when it was acquired by Joshua Tetley & Son. Although some modification has been carried out, much of the original wood interior is still preserved.

Perhaps one of the most curious features of the pub is its name or rather the confusion of what the name really is. The *York Directory* of 1885 clearly gives it as the Swan Inn but in deeds of 1881 it is referred to as the White

Swan Inn and this confusion was repeated in a sale of 1887 when the conveyance refers to the Swan Inn and other documents call it the White Swan. To add to the confusion a mortgage of 1881 refers to it as the Swan Inn and associated sale documents call it the Swann Inn. If it really was the Swann Inn originally then it seems likely that it took the name from the Swann family who gave their name to nearby Swann Street.

However there is one intriguing possibility to account for the origin of the Swan's name which is the spelling most frequently used in various documents, and that lies back in the pub's origins as a beer-house. At Christmas 1857, not long after Thomas Staverley opened up his premises, seven cygnets, which had been a star attraction at the annual city Fatstock and Poultry Show, were bought by public subscription and presented to the Corporation to establish a colony of swans on the River Ouse. Since the river is only at the bottom of Clementhorpe it might have been considered both topical and appropriate to name the new pub The Swan after its newest neighbours.

Cross and turn right to continue along Bishopthorpe Road past a street called Clementhorpe on your left. Half way down this, running parallel with Bishopthorpe Road, is Cherry Street at the corner of which in 1851 was discovered a large part of a well-preserved mosaic. One end was uncovered and found to comprise an area eleven feet by eight feet decorated with various coloured geometrical patterns and shapes.

Continue forward through the whole area, which is known as Clementhorpe. The name was in use in 1070 long before St Clement's Priory was founded here by Archbishop Thurstan about 1130. He "granted to God, St. Clement and the nuns of St Clement, the place on which their house was erected, together with two carucates* of land in the suburbs of York, and twenty shillings issuing from a fair in York". This was a considerable area on your left.

The Priory from its foundation was an independent house, under the jurisdiction of no abbey, but subject only to the Archbishop of York, and when Archbishop Geoffrey in 1192 attempted to lower the status of the house, Prioress Alicia went to Rome and made an appeal to the Pope. Though the Archbishop disregarded the appeal and excommunicated all the sisters, their cause eventually triumphed and the independence of the Nunnery was maintained.

Its affairs as recorded have a more secular tinge of life and the reputation

---

*　　two carucates = twice as much land as a team of oxen could plough in a season of the nuns not the most saintly; probably they were more human than spiritual, for the sisters seem to have mixed with the world rather freely. Their hospitality was widely known, and the privilege seems to have been abused. On 24 March 1312 the abbot and monks of Selby were prohibited from visiting Clementhorpe or spending the night there, the social attractions evidently having been strongly in evidence to call forth this censure from the archbishop.

Isabel Warde was the last prioress and she was compelled to sell a silver chalice and cup together with some reliquaries to meet the extra expenses incurred when the Commissioners of Henry VIII arrived at the Nunnery on 13 June 1536 for the Dissolution and disbanding of the community which was completed by 31 August. In the eighteenth century some of the ruins were in existence and in 1903 a small portion of the close wall was standing near the bottom of the street called Clementhorpe but that last fragment has been swept away for dwelling-houses.

On your right stood Bishop's Chapel which was erected to commemorate the death of Archbishop Scrope who was executed on 8 June 1405. The site of the chapel was on the very field, possibly on the exact spot where he was beheaded. The location is described by one historian as being near Bishopthorpe; by the famous antiquary Francis Drake as being between Bishopthorpe and York; and by John Browne quoting from Clement Maydstone, the son of a contemporary of the Archbishop, as "in a field by Clementhorpe, near York". The various descriptions are not contradictory, Browne simply being more precise than the others. The exact spot would be on the west side of Bishopthorpe Road, probably on land now occupied by houses numbered 75 to 81. There are no remains of the chapel but land on which the houses stand and Nunmill Street behind is still known as "Chapel Fields".

Continue forward until you reach Richardson Street where you should turn left to enter Rowntree Park given to the city by the Rowntree family as a memorial to the staff killed in the First World War. Either continue forward or explore the park, but exit by the gates ahead into Terry Avenue, alongside the River Ouse.

Turn right and follow the tree-lined narrow road along the banks and ignore the right hand bend up Butcher Terrace to proceed forward along the cycle and pathway beside the river through Nun Ings.

Cross a couple of stiles before reaching a narrow track which turns right through a gateway to rejoin Bishopthorpe Road. Turn right up the slope past the tree-shrouded crematorium on your right to go over the outer bypass and drop down to Middlethorpe Hall on your right. This imposing three-storeyed brick structure was built about 1702 for Thomas Barlow, a

Sheffield master cutler, and is surmounted by stone eagles taken from the family coat of arms which was granted in 1691. He bought the manor of Middlethorpe in 1698. Antiquarian Ralph Thoresby's diary records that on 17 September 1702 he "received a visit from Mr Barlow of Middlethorp near York, which very curious house he built after the Italian mode". This too was briefly the home of Lady Mary Wortley Montague, the brilliant chronicler of eighteenth century life. She travelled widely, observed acutely and wrote sheaves of letters some of which emanated from Middelethorpe Hall. Today it survives as a luxury hotel.

John Carr's racecourse stand.

In 1812 some leaden bullets and steel breast plates were found in Middlethorpe. These may have been relics from the Scottish contingent of Cromwell's army who were encamped here when attacking York. There was a bridge of boats over the River Ouse and constant communication with Roundheads quartered on the other side at Fulford.

Cross the road here to go around a white gate and enter Green Lane. To your right you will see the former Knavesmire School on a 13-acre site which in 1989 became a College of Law for about 600 post graduate students seeking to become solicitors.

The lane crosses the long straight of the race-course to join a combined cycle and walkway which swings left around the edge of Middlethorpe Wood at the end of Micklegate Stray.— the largest of the city's strays which from time immemorial have belonged to the freemen of the city — and is dominated by the Knavesmire race-course.

As its name implies, the Knavesmire was a swamp with a stream running through it, but after considerable levelling and draining the course was made in the shape of a horseshoe in time for the first meeting which was held in 1731 with prize money of £155 for a five-day meeting.

Prior to that date, horses were matched against each other on Clifton

Ings, and the House Book of York Corporation records that the City supported racing there for the first time in 1530, although the first detailed record of a race meeting dates from 1709. In addition, racing is known to have taken place on the frozen River Ouse between Micklegate Tower and Skeldergate Postern in 1607, and in 1633 King Charles I, during a visit to York, witnessed a horse race on Acomb Moor.

Unfortunately Clifton Ings was subject to frequent flooding so racing was transferred to the Knavesmire but there were no permanent buildings there until the first Grand Stand, designed by the city's famous architect John Carr, was erected by subscription in 1753. The arcade of this building was subsequently re-erected in 1907 in the paddock where it still remains dominated by the more modern stand built in 1965. An even newer five-storey stand containing a suite of twenty-seven exclusive boxes and accommodation for a further 800 punters and costing £2.5 million was completed in 1989.

When you reach Sim Balk Lane turn right and walk forward up the gentle slope to the junction with Tadcaster Road where you again turn right.

Almost immediately on your right you will pass a city boundary board decorated with the coat of arms topped by the 'Cap of Maintenance' which is a reminder that this is a well trodden royal route from the south. The first Cap of Maintenance was, according to tradition, presented to the Lord Mayor Robert Savage by King Richard II in 1393 — a claim which cannot be authenticated but is probably correct as Richard II and his court appear to have moved to York in 1392. The first mention in the city archives is in 1442/3 when sevenpence was spent on repairs to the Mayor's hat, as it was then called. The earliest use of the term 'Cap of Maintenance' is in a record of 1580 when reference is made to "the hatte of maytenance that the sword berer doth weare at certain tymes".

The grass verges on the approach and under the tree-lined cycle track on your left, opposite the sixth form college, are carpeted in spring with narcissus or daffodils as they are more commonly called. Narcissus went down in history as the youth whose punishment for being a cold-hearted swine was to fall in love with his reflection — and pine away and die. But in true Greek tradition the story did not end there. In death he was transformed into the flower which still bears his name. Poets write of them, tourists come visiting to see them, and gardeners recognise them as the true harbingers of spring echoing the old rhyme:

Daffy-down-dilly is come up to town
In her yellow petticoat
And her green gown.

Just after passing the decorative cobbled frontage of Chessingham Gardens on your right you will see an old milestone which records that you are at Dringhouses on the Tadcaster and Hob Moor Road some 7 miles from Tadcaster, 21 miles from Leeds and, with unusual attention to fractional accuracy, 2½ miles from York.

Keep forward past York College of Further Education which incorporates the Ashfield property of Sir Lycett Green, a Wakefield engineering family that owed its fortunes to a "fuel economiser" which enabled a considerable saving in the consumption of coal through a comparatively simple engineering device. He was Master of the York and Ainsty Hunt from 1886 to 1909, owned a number of racehorses named after local landmarks, and invented a golf competition known as a "Greensome".

Legend has it that on one hot summer day, Lady Green, who was a strong temperance advocate, brought out some soft drinks for a crew threshing corn. The men were somewhat displeased until the Squire came along and with the remark: "All right, she's gone! You can't work on that stuff", produced some crates of ale which he had hidden nearby.

On another occasion, when one of his grooms was reported for being drunk, Sir Lycett promptly sacked him but the man was little concerned as it was well known as the squire's normal way of letting off steam. The groom was told that if he had to get drunk he should find a less noticeable way home and Sir Lycett gave him some cash to do a dummy run. The route should have involved crossing the beck by a plank but the unfortunate groom eventually arrived back in his stocking feet and an apprentice had to be despatched next day to retrieve his boots out of the mud at the bottom of the beck.

Over on your left is Aldersyde, a large house which once belonged to Mr Ernest Leetham of Hungate Flour Mills before being sold and converted into flats and the grounds built over.

Another big house was

Milestone at Dringhouses.

Dringthorpe which was the home of Colonel Sir Charles Read, whose gardener gave us the Russell lupin. After occupation by the army in the Second World War it became a Blind Home and was finally demolished to make way for the Wilberforce Home for the Multiply Handicapped Blind which you pass on your right.

Continue through the old village of Dringhouses. Known in 1109 as Drengeshires it means "the houses of the drengs", a dreng being a warrior landholder with possessions granted by the Viking leader Hafdan who was victorious in AD876. In 1937 York City Council decided to extend its boundaries to include Dringhouses as well as Middlethorpe and Acomb. Almost half a century earlier, in 1876, a local public meeting had resolved that "Captain Heath, as Senior Church Warden, should unite with other parishes in adopting any measures that he may think fit to frustrate the attempts to attach Dringhouses to the City of York for either Parliamentary or Municipal purposes".

Soon you pass on your left number 100, a large house called Tollgarth built in 1910 which stands on the site of the old toll house demolished five years earlier. After a meeting in 1724 of landed gentry and York Corporation, an Act of Parliament had been passed authorising the conversion of the York-Tadcaster Road into a turnpike with a single gate being erected not more than three miles from York and tolls charged for road maintenance.

The row of shops also on your left were originally cottages known as Meek's Buildings, nick-named "Washing Tub Row" because those who lived there took in washing for the gentry.

Further forward and on your right you will see a rare brick pinfold or pound on part of a grassed area which was once the village green. Enclosures such as this were put up by local authorities so that cattle caught straying or doing damage could be penned up until a fine or payment for damages had been worked out. Although most villages used to

Fox Hotel, Tadcaster Road.

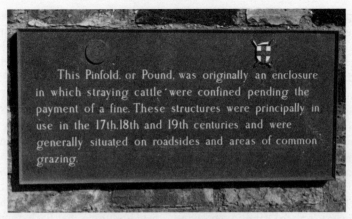

This Pinfold, or Pound, was originally an enclosure in which straying cattle were confined pending the payment of a fine. These structures were principally in use in the 17th,18th and 19th centuries and were generally situated on roadsides and areas of common grazing.

Pinfold plaque at Dringhouses.

have one there seems to be no record of when or by whom it was built. The only other local pinfold was planned for Tang Hall in the early seventeenth century, but it is not recorded on a map of 1634.

The Fox Hotel on your left was bought on 21 November 1873 by William Clark Yates from Ciceley Bulmer and it was acquired on 16 July 1875 by Tadcaster Tower Brewery which became part of Bass North Ltd.

Next to it is the public library which served as the village school from 1852, having been formed in 1849 in a room next to the church. The manager received a small Government grant, fees were charged (threepence for a senior and twopence for a junior) and attendance was not compulsory. In 1902 the school came under the West Riding Education Committee and in 1904 was moved to its present site in St Helen's Road.

In 1863, a master recorded that many children were away gathering fruit and on 13 November school was "thin" because most of the older boys were lifting potatoes. On 9 December 1875 the master recorded: "Attendance continues to be lamentably irregular, many of the boys' mothers take in washing, and they are continually employed in carrying clothes". And in November 1878 only three children came to school because of "a tremendous snowstorm", whilst in January 1881 the ink was frozen and slates had to be used.

Discipline was strict with boys being flogged for telling lies and in 1890 a boy was punished "for impertinence to the Vicar during the Catechism lesson".

The Post House Hotel on your right, opened on 29 September 1971, stands on the site of the former Manor House and was designed around a 200-year-old cedar tree. It now also boasts two rare redwood trees which

Steel sculpture at the Post House Hotel.

can grow up to 150 feet high. Until forty-six years ago the dawn redwood, a deciduous conifer, was only known through fossil remains and was thought to be extinct. In 1941 specimens were found growing in a remote valley in China. The tree gets its name from the colour of its leaves which turn a stunning red in autumn. At the corner of the gardens is a novel piece of stainless steel sculpture.

In the fifteenth century this was the manor of Francis, Viscount Lovel, personal friend and faithful adherent of Richard, Duke of Gloucester, afterwards King Richard III. From this association was derived the doggerel lines :

The catte, the ratte, and Lovel our dogge,
Rulyth all England under a hogge

The animals were symbols in the coats of arms of Catesby, Ratclyffe and Lovel.

In the latter part of the reign of King Edward IV, Richard Carbett who was Lovel's tenant at the Dringhouses manor house, was accustomed to pasture his cattle upon Knavesmire, to the chagrin of the freemen of York who claimed the grazing rights of the Stray.

The dispute claimed the attention of the City fathers and on 13 August 1479 Lord Lovel, attended by his counsel, came to York to uphold the rights of his representative. Unwilling to concede, yet loth to offend the powerful noble, the magistrates allowed the matter to drift for four years. However when it became known that King Richard III was on his way to York, with Lord Lovel in his train as Lord Chamberlain of his household, the Corporation rapidly reached their decision. They made an order:

"that it should be answered to the counsel of my Lord Lovel that the Mayor and his brethren would not be against the right of my said Lord, but would be agreeable that he should have his right, so that none other of Drynghows have common in the said pasture, but only the tenant of my said Lord Lovel of his

chief place there, to the number of twenty kyne and a bull, so that the said tenant have none of other man's beasts to gest, but occupy the common with his own beasts, and that his beasts have a mark that they may be known from others."

At the corner next to the piece of steel art is a small stone inscribed "Boundary of St Edward's Vicarage" and the parish church of St Edward the Confessor which replaced an earlier one dedicated to St Helen about 1482. Opposite is St Helen's Road made in 1902. St Helen was a popular saint in Yorkshire, because her son, Constantine the Great, had been proclaimed Emperor in York, where his father died on his return from a campaign against the Picts. One legend suggests that Helen was Romano-British, but this was not true. She was the daughter of an inn-keeper in a Balkans garrison town where she met, and may have married, Constantine's father. He was a Roman officer who evidently had the necessary mixture of good fortune, guile, and ruthlessness to become a Roman Emperor. Helen became a saint because she backed her son in his support of the clergy and built a church on the Mount of Olives.

On 28 April 1704 the famous Leeds antiquary Ralph Thoresby passed this way and recorded: "E'er I was well begun on my journey I got a sharp shower that drove me into the church porch at Dringhouses. I was troubled to see an ale house at one end and a tavern at the other joined close to the edifice".

In 1725 a new church was built by Francis Barlow, Lord of the Manor (son of Thomas Barlow of Middlethorpe Hall). This was replaced at a cost of £500 by Francis Leigh with the foundation stone being laid in November 1847 and consecration being on 8 August 1849. That was the birthday of Edward Leigh and, in memory of her husband, Francis Leigh had the church dedicated to St Edward the Confessor, the pious, if politically inept, Saxon King from 1042-1066 who founded the first Westminster Abbey. Designed by Vickers and Hugall of Pontefract, St Edward's looks like the original, although the spire is now of fibreglass!

On the corner of St Helen's Road is the Cross Keys Inn which was bought on 21 November 1899 from the "Masters in Lunacy", acting on behalf of Robert Danby who had taken it over on 20 July 1879, by the John J Hunt Brewery which eventually became part of J.W. Cameron & Co Ltd. Behind the inn, on what has become the car park, was stabling for fifteen horses where Army officers from Fulford kept their polo ponies for playing on Knavesmire before the Second World War. After that, the stables were used by a succession of racehorse trainers until the buildings were demolished. However the Cross Keys can claim to be one of the oldest inns as an early record describes the payment of "20 pence for my lords' drinking at

Rynghouses" when Edward Prince of Wales, son of Richard III, called at the inn in 1483 on his way from the family castle at Middleham. A two-horse bus service with a fare of threepence operated in 1897 from here to Pavement in the city.

Attracting attention on your right is the giant saddle sign of the Swallow

St Edwards church, Dringhouses.

Chase Hotel. This was originally a private house called 'The Hollies' owned by Major Close of the Steel Works Forge in Leeman Road, built for him by the North Eastern Railway Company in exchange for his previous home which stood on the site now occupied by the Royal York Hotel. The property was acquired in the twenties by Mrs Rasdal and Mrs Witham who ran Harker's Hotel which formerly stood on the site of Betty's Restaurant in St Helen's Square — the starting point in coaching days for the mails — and they transferred the name. After the Second World War it became 'The Chase' and was renamed in 1988 when acquired by Swallow Hotels.

Early illustrations of Romans mounted show them seated on what they termed *ephippium*. This was more than a mere cloth or skin, for it had a frame of wood, covered and stuffed, the whole being secured by a girth. One authority says: "After the overthrow of the Roman Empire we find stirrups in use and men rode in huge war saddles, so trussed up that getting into them was difficult and falling out almost impossible". By the reign of James I both York and Ripon were famed for the saddle trees their craftsmen turned out and for long racehorses carried heavy weights — 10-12 stones — so there was no call for light racing saddles so essential now.

This was once the York boundary — Dringhouses was a West Riding village. By 1911 electric tramcars started from here, running on a single track into the city, with a loop line at Hob Moor gates to allow trams going in the opposite direction to pass: they went as far as Fulford Cross which is now Unwins Garage. By 1935 their was a tram every 7½ minutes for the twopenny journey to the city, when the service was discontinued.

On your left is Ainsty Grove leading to Ainsty Avenue at the end of which is Nelson's pond — one of four excavations by clay diggers once engaged in the village's main industry of brick and tile making. Now it serves as a useful amenity for British Rail Staff Association.

Continue along the tree-lined road with splendid views across the Knavesmire, for long a marshy, undrained bog, which explains its name, according to a nineteenth century writer. He says:

"Anciently the word knave did not bear its present opprobrious significance. The Anglo-Saxon, cnap: Belgic, knape: and Teutonic, knab, meant formerly a menial servant or poor householder. A mire is a low watery piece of ground; so that this common (which is in some parts very soft in wet weather) had its name from that for which it was originally intended, & is still intended; viz. for the benefit of the poor freemen of the city, as a common for what cattle they can put on it. The

inhabitants of Dringhouses and Middlethorpe have both laid claim to this property, and, in the city's registers are various entries on the subject. Ultimately they were allowed to participate to a certain extent, and, to this day (1842) they have the right of pasturage for a limited number of cattle".

Alongside the fence on your right opposite the Knavesmire Manor Hotel you will pass another of the old turnpike milestones which gives its position as 'York City' although it also informs observers they are 1½ miles from York.

Soon you reach on your right the raised stone platform with its commemorative obelisk which marks the site of Tyburn, named in imitation of its London counterpart. Here was where Master Joseph Penny, joiner of Blake Street was instructed in 1379 "to build the said gallows forthwith at a cost of £10/15s", for the execution of criminals, and it continued to serve its grisly purpose until 1802 when one was erected outside York Castle.

Hanged here was Richard Turpin in 1739 and murderer Eugene Aram in 1759 as well as numerous others less notorious. Turpin went to the gibbet splendidly dressed, wearing a new fustian coat purchased the day before. He paid five poor men ten shillings each to walk behind the cart which was to bear his body. On 10 April 1739 he was hanged but he kept his executioner talking for half an hour. The corpse was taken to the Blue Boar pub in Castlegate and was buried the following day in St George's churchyard. Body snatchers stole it the same night but it was found in a doctor's garden and reburied in quicklime.

This spot too has sacred associations for Roman Catholics because of their co-religionists who met their death here in the reign of Queen Elizabeth I. But no one seems to remember Valentine Freez, who was admitted to the freedom of the city in 1539, and opposite whose name in the city register of freemen is written *Combustus erat Knavesmire propter heresem* (He was burned near Knavesmire on account of heresy — that is, the reformed faith). Apparently his wife shared his fate for, according to one account, "They were both born in the city and both gave their lives at one stake for the testimony of Jesus Christ".

In contrast, the Knavesmire was also the setting for one of the most remarkable racing stories and possibly a sporting "double" when the crowd witnessed the first woman to ride in a bona-fide horse race and the first negro fighter take to the boxing ring.

Born a slave at Staten Island in 1763, negro Bill Richmond had gained some success with his fists before being brought to Britain to work as a servant and subsequently apprenticed to a York cabinet maker. It was not until 1804 at the age of 41 that he "started his famous fistic career in the

Minster city" according to the *York Gazette*. Following disparaging re-
marks by a fighter named George Moore about the colour of Richmond's
skin and rainbow clothes, "they set to there and then" according to the
newspaper report, and twenty-five minutes were all that Richmond
needed to change Moore's opinion of black fighters. "And two of Moore's
pals took the knockout too" readers were told.

But the main attraction that had brought 100,000 people to the Knavesmire that day was the appearance of the flamboyant Mrs T — Alicia
Thornton — to ride in her losing but ever-famous match against celebrated
sportsman Captain Flint over a four mile stretch. Alicia Meynell adopted
the surname Thornton from her benefactor Colonel Thomas Thornton of
Thornton Royal near Knaresborough. She led the race for three miles when
her horse fell lame and Flint won, but the matter was not allowed to rest
there.

Alicia demanded a re-match with Flint whose attitude was summed up
in verse:

> To your challenge anew I beg to reply,
> When your ladyship's made every bet,
> I'll be proud to attend, the contest to try,
> For the honour again of your wit.

The Colonel couldn't, or wouldn't, settle his account with Flint over the
first match so Flint not surprisingly refused the re-match and there was
ill-feeling between the three of them. Infuriated by the Colonel's refusal
to hand over the thousand pounds which had been wagered, Flint horse-
whipped the Colonel while Alicia went on to win a challenge with another
opponent before disappearing from the York scene leaving a trail of chaos
and Thornton and Flint still at loggerheads.

From Tyburn walk diagonally to your left to cross Knavesmire Road near
some toilets and then follow the path along the edge of some allotments
to reach a stone flight of steps. Climb these and go through the iron stile,
cross Albemarle Road and go through another iron stile to follow the path
which weaves its way through allotments each with its vegetables, fruit
or flowers reflecting the individuality of the gardeners. Exit through a
wooden gate to cross Scarcroft Road, with property little changed in
almost a century, and walk diagonally left along the concrete path across
the green playing field outside Scarcroft Road school built in 1896 with
steep roofs. Turrets run up the corners of the central block, and a large
turret with a clock tops the whole composition of what is one of the city's
grandest buildings, designed by Walter Brierley. At the corner where the
arched gateway is inscribed GIRLS ENTRANCE follow the wall on your
right and go forward to cross Moss Street.

Enter the narrow Scarcroft Lane and as you walk forward, opposite a doorway marked No 2 on your left, look for an ancient metal plaque on the wall on your right with the message: "This Wall & Carriage Road belong exclusively to the Freemen of Micklegate Ward".

In a document produced during the reign of Henry VIII there is an accurate description of the former condition of this locality. Scarcroft is Carr-croft, the term Carr being a common word for low marshy land.

Continue forward to join Nunnery Lane alongside the Trafalgar Bay pub whose signboard reminds you that the famous battle was fought on 21 October 1805. Turn right and on the corner of Dale Street notice the doorway with the glass panel above lettered "Bottle & Jug" which is a relic of the days when it served as a pub and had an outsales activity. Pass on your right Swann Street and the Victoria Vaults pub where you cross to the Moat Hotel to complete your walk. In the central eave of this white-brick Dutch-gabled building is a stone panel inscribed "St Thomas's Hospital Re-Built AD1862" commemorating the removal of the hospital here from Micklegate when road widening caused the original hospital to be demolished in 1863. It ceased to function about 1969 and after being derelict for about two years it was converted into the present hotel.

8

Meet the Three-legged Mare
MICKLEGATE BAR

Micklegate Bar — Blossom Street — The Mount — Mount Vale —
Tadcaster Road — Hob Moor — Green Lane — Hamilton Drive West —
West Bank Park — Windmill Rise — Poppleton Road — Holgate Road —
Wilton Rise — Cinder Lane — Leeman Road — Station Rise —
Station Road — Queen Street — Micklegate Bar.

approx. 4 miles

ALMOST EVERY SOVEREIGN that has reigned over England since William the Conqueror to Queen Elizabeth II has passed through Micklegate Bar — the principal and most important gateway commanding the road to London. When Henry VIII was expected it was decked with his arms and those of Catherine Howard and Prince Edward, but in fact the King entered the city by Walmgate Bar.

Probably the earliest reference to the existence of Micklegate Bar is the granting of a licence in 1196 to one Benedict Englesan to build a house on the Bar. He paid half a mark for a building licence and an annual rent of sixpence for having it hereditary. Since Norman times it has been used as rooms for the gate-sergeant, a tenement for retiring aldermen, a prison, and more recently by a fencing club.

Formerly called Micklelith or the great gate, it incorporates a twelfth century gritstone outer arch, and the walls of the passage are built of re-used Roman stonework, including coffins. The gate-house has lofty turrets with figures of knights and the facade bears, under a helm with lion crest, the royal arms of Edward III; two shields of the city arms; and also the arms of Lord Mayor, Sir John Lister-Kaye commemorating an eighteenth century repair.

The severed heads or quarters of traitors and rebels were displayed on pikes here because it was the most frequented city gate. The heads of Sir Henry Percy (Hotspur) in 1403, of Richard, Duke of York in 1460, of Lancastrian leaders captured at the Battle of Towton in 1461, of the Earl of Northumberland in 1572, of Puritan conspirators in 1663, and of Jacobites in 1746 — all these and many others were piked on poles above the Bar. Not until 1754 did the practice cease when the last two heads were stolen by Jacobite tailor William Arundell to the great indignation of the Government. He was caught, sentenced to two years in jail and a fine of

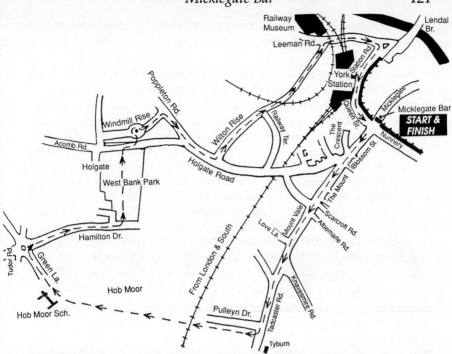

£5. Perhaps that is why it boasts several ghosts, including an amiable gentleman in a black cloak.

On 20 March 1989 an exhibition was officially opened in the Bar as a dedication to the ill-fated monarch King Richard III. The head of his brother Edmund, Earl of Rutland, was piked here with that of his father who, Shakespeare tells us, wore a paper crown so "that York may overlook York". The exhibition includes a framed resumé of Richard's life; a backcloth bearing his symbol, the white boar; a copy of Richard's charter to the city of York; and a replica of the famous Middleham jewel. After the siege of the city in 1644 the Royalist garrison of about a thousand were given safe conduct to Skipton. They marched out of Micklegate Bar with drums beating and colours flying through the ranks of the victorious Roundheads.

With the bar behind you, on your left is the Punch Bowl Hotel standing on the site of the Hospital of St Thomas of Canterbury, first recorded in 1391, its purpose being the maintenance of the poor and the provision of hospitality for travellers. St Thomas's was transferred to the Corpus Christi Guild in 1478, survived the Dissolution which closed so many York religious houses in the sixteenth century, and was finally demolished in 1863 when the road was widened. A three-storeyed shop with a curved corner was then built on the site and occupied by a chemist followed by a succession of butchers before being incorporated into the next door Punch Bowl Hotel.

Walk forward into Blossom Street. In an account of the receiver of rents for the See of York in the reign of King Edward III, and in some fourteenth century documents, this street is called "Ploxom Gate". In the succeeding century the name had been suffixed to "Ploughs-wain-gate", which some authorities suggest means the ploughman's street. A garden in Ploughs-wain-gate in the suburbs of the city was part of the dower lands of Margaret, the widow of Sir Richard Scrope of Bolton who lived in the reign of King Henry V. Two centuries more pass and we find "An orchard and a dove-cote on Blossom Gate, otherwise Plaxholme Gate" which were the property of Michael Lowick in the second year of King James I. And twenty years later in 1624 Thomas Campleshon sold a house in "Ploxwain-gate, otherwise Blossom gate, without Micklegate Bar, in the suburbs of the city of York".

The street is a thousand years older than the thirteenth century, for this is the Roman route to Calcaria (Tadcaster) and the south of England. Indeed, until 1792, when Selby bridge was built because there was no other River Ouse crossing between Ouse Bridge and the sea, it was the only main road to London.

Immediately on your left is the imposing Bar Convent which celebrated its tricentenary in 1986 and has been converted into a museum. Permanent displays outline the early history of Christianity in the North of England leading to the story of Mary Ward, the Yorkshire woman who founded the worldwide Institute of the Blessed Virgin Mary of which the Bar Convent is one of the earliest houses still in existence.

Founded in 1686, the origin of the building was a small house bought with a gift from Sir Thomas Gascoigne. It housed a poor school and boarding establishment for the daughters of Catholics.

A century later, work was completed on the present building with its glass-fronted and elaborately tiled front hall and cast iron furniture from Coalbrookdale. The new school boasted an elegant Georgian facade hiding the illegal Catholic community behind its walls.

The most elegant piece of camouflage was provided by the magnificent neo-classical chapel. Its grand domed roof was hidden from the view of the outside world by a second roof built over its decorated curves. Nuns running the school also went incognito, discarding the habit for everyday clothes.

Languages were a strong feature of the timetable of the day, but the pioneering school also taught mathematics. The radical approach was in the tradition of the order's founder, Mary Ward.

Born in Ripon and the niece of two conspirators in the Gunpowder Plot, the young nun clashed regularly with Rome in her efforts to take her sisters away from the cloistered life of the convent and into the community. The library reflects this with books used by the highly educated nuns over three centuries and archive material disclosing the everyday facts of their life — their vows, their letters, their accounts, and their recipes.

The Bar Convent sitting outside the walls was a practical choice because it was thought to be more healthy, but whether this was because it was then really in the country or because of the fact that Catholic churches were still outlawed is not at all certain.

Lendal Bridge and Esplanade.

Sisters with this order found friends with other "rebels" in the area at the time, and the clock at the front of the building was made by Henry Hindley who probably never saw his timepiece in place. He was a Jacobite and so whenever he wanted to travel outside the city he had to get a special Movement Order.

Henry Hindley, who became one of the most respected clockmakers in the country, came to York from Wigan in the 1720s. He served his apprenticeship and then became a journeyman, but the only way to become a freeman and establish a business inside the city walls was to secure some patronage. Two superb grandfather clocks presented to the Lord Mayor ensured Hindley becoming a freeman and he went on to make Gog and Magog in the Minster as well as hundreds of other timepieces of all shapes and sizes.

Opposite is the seventeenth century Windmill Inn, known by its present name since 1735 when the heirs of Henry Lee sold it to the occupier. For at least four generations from 1621 the Lee family had been millers at one of the windmills on The Mount and it is doubtless from this link that the inn took its name. More recently is has been the setting for some ghostly activity. Sounds of feet climbing wooden stairs have been heard despite the presence of thick carpeting; lights have mysteriously been switched on and off in cellars and storerooms even when the building has been thoroughly checked and locked for security; and in the same circumstances glasses and bottles have been shattered. Apparently a manager and barman have found themselves assailed by icy cold mist inside, and an ostler in eighteenth century costume is alleged to have been seen. An old book about the city is said to contain a story that the inn is haunted by the spirit of a little girl knocked down and killed by a brewer's dray many years ago.

Before the modern Prudential building is the York Railwaymen's Club built as a pair of houses with a large warehouse behind by wine merchant John Horner in 1789. Among distinguished residents who lived here was the first Joseph Rowntree (1801-59), and between 1807 and 1831 architects Charles Watson and James Pigott Pritchett .

A venture of the York Commercial Building Company in 1824/8 created the twenty fine houses of the long terrace called South Parade on your left. First occupier of number 17 was architect Peter Atkinson, and next door in number 16 was builder Thomas Rayson, both of whom were responsible for the properties.

Opposite, on your right, is the Odeon cinema with its massive tower block relieved by pilasters. Built in 1936/7 it is listed as a building of special architectural interest and is regarded by many as the best work of cinema designer Harry Weedon.

The cobbled strips at the sides of the road once provided space for a horse and cattle market and there may have also been a hiring fair for servants.

Possibly built originally as a farmhouse, following the siege of York, the Bay Horse is a typical Victorian inn and served as such before the middle of the eighteenth century. Its sign is first mentioned in 1798 and may refer to the racehorse *Bay Malton* which in 1765 won the famous Gimcrack 500 guineas at York. George Benson, the architect and local historian, was the son of a former landlord and spent his childhood here. An unusual item on one of the pewter-topped bars is a gold changer, an object rather like a gas meter from which change was obtained for gold sovereigns. And a little six-inch square spy hole has been retained so an observer can peep from one room into another.

Outside, on the corner of Shaw Terrace with a horse's head in relief, is a plaque which tells passers-by:

The Cleveland Bay dates back to before the seventeenth century. When travel by coach became popular during Elizabethan times, Clevelands renowned for their stamina and active pace were used as harness horses. The breed continued to flourish both as coach horse and as an agricultural horse particularly in its native Yorkshire. Industrialisation led to its decline until in 1962 only nine pure stallions remained.

Across Blossom Street is The Crescent built in 1868/9 on land behind which used to stand the timbered range of almshouses called Barstow's Hospital, replaced by shops in the nineteenth century. In the second house lived the Reverend James Raine, chancellor of the Minster and historian.

Proceed past Holgate Road, once Holgate Lane, on your right, to The Mount public house which boasts over the entrance an ornate gas lamp which still works. On your left is the Abbey Park Hotel which has been much extended but preserves the fine brick house designed by Peter Atkinson (1776-1843) and built in 1832 for Alderman William Dunslay. The main frontage is on to Park Street where the first house on the left was built for his own use by bricklayer and building contractor Thomas Rayson in 1836.

Most of the houses hereabouts were built for professional men and artisans. On the site surrounded by gilt topped iron railings, which is now the offices of Shepherd Homes at Number 89, was the home of John Dales, Lord Mayor in 1816 and 1829, which he probably built and called it 'The Cottage'. Later it was the home of well-known land agent and philanthropist James Clutton. Opposite is number 98 where lived two sisters of York artist Henry Cave, and in number 102 there lived for a time Elizabeth Frank, the friend and biographer of the Quaker grammarian Lindley Murray.

The road here was the setting for a tragic tale commemorated by a small weather-worn monument near the vestry door of Holy Trinity church in Micklegate.

The story started between eight and nine o'clock on the evening of Saturday 15 October 1768 when the London to York stage-coach was travelling along the Mount towards Micklegate Bar.

Readers of the *York Courant* were told a few days later that the coach was *"overturned within a quarter of a mile of this city by the driver's endeavouring to pass the Fly, whereby, the coachman had his left leg broken and shattered in such a manner that it was obliged to be immediately cut off, and a young man, who was on the box with him, was killed. There were in the coach one man, four women and a young child who received little hurt".*

The young man — he was only nineteen — came from Morpeth and was buried at Holy Trinity. At this time the coach, which departed at the chilling hour of 2.00am, completed the London/York run in two days and

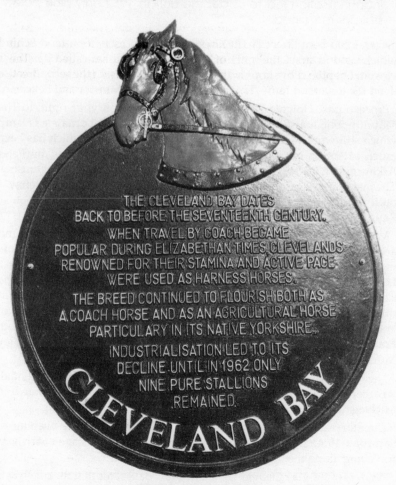

Cleveland Bay plaque.

passengers were charged threepence a mile

Just past Scarcroft Road, on the site now occupied by houses numbered 120-4 and the gardens behind next to Mount Parade on your right, stood St Katherine's Hospital founded about 1333. Its purpose was revealed a year later with the request: "Protection for one year for leprous men of the Hospital of St Katherine. Drynhous, seeking alms for the support of their house". The hospital was taken down and rebuilt in 1652 but in 1835 was so dilapidated that it was demolished.

Stopping many passers-by in their tracks is the black stone cat sat on a window ledge of number 105 on your left. This is the trade mark of architect Tom Adams which perches on his drawings, publicity literature, site boards and now appears on strategic vantage points of buildings with which he has been associated, including his offices here. The cats, in various postures, are all the work of York sculptor Jonathan Newdick. The first went onto the ridge of a new shopping development in Coney Street, and the highest must be on the penthouse development in King's Square.

'Nunroyd' and houses on the Mount.

Sandwiched between Mill Mount Court and Mill Mount Lane on your left at number 109 is a house with full-height bays in a late-Georgian front. Named 'Nunroyd' it was rebuilt in 1797 and enlarged in 1911 by the then Lord Mayor, Norman Green. One of its occupiers was herald-painter Thomas Hungate who inherited a baronetcy in 1749. He did not use the title "being a man of penurious habits and of reserved and singular manners". Other occupiers included widowed Mrs Beningfield, grandmother of eccentric naturalist traveller Charles Waterton.

Mill Mount Court and Mill Mount Lane are reminders that for many years a wooden post mill stood hereabouts on the brow of the hill before it drops down Mount Vale to become Tadcaster Road. Despite its importance this route has not always been easily passable for, in April 1742, the Corporation had to appoint a committee to direct and superintend the levelling of the Mount to make a safe and convenient road which they managed to do for £50; but in 1753 it was found necessary to drain off a spring which flowed through the road here.

Across the road is a short terrace of five houses numbered 136-44 built in 1824 on a field called Shepherds Close which belonged to the parish estate of Holy Trinity in Micklegate.

Cross Albemarle Road as you proceed forward, and fading lettering on the stone gateposts of the Mount Royale Hotel reveals that it is a combination of Beech House and Daresbury House in whose front gardens once stood the chapel of St James' — one of the first to be erected in York. This was founded by one Roger the priest about the beginning of the reign of King Stephen (1135-1154). The land, which also covered part of the existing roadway, was then at the "stone cross outside the west gate of the city" and given to the monks of Holy Trinity, Micklegate on condition that they caused divine service to be performed there "without intermission".

King Stephen granted to this chapel the land on which the thieves' gallows stood, *extra portam civitatis* (outside the city wall), and this probably eventually became the site of the Knavesmire Tyburn. A gruesome link occurred in 1280 when a man called Elenstring was hanged for larceny and his body was brought to St James' Chapel for burial. On arrival he was found to be alive and was then pardoned.

The chapel was the first anyone approaching from the south would encounter and being opposite the "stone cross" where pilgrims would make their devotions it became famous as the point to which a new bishop came to be enthroned in the Minster. The Dean and Chapter would meet him here and the Archbishop elect would probably pray at the stone cross after which the religious ceremony would begin in the chapel. Then he would walk barefoot to the Minster. A cloth, however, was laid down for him to walk over and this was afterwards cut up and given to the poor women of the city; one writer amplifying this statement by saying "to make petticoats of!".

By 1651 the chapel was in ruins and in 1736 the last portion of the foundations was removed.

Over the years numerous discoveries on the Mount confirm that it was part of an avenue of memorials to the Roman dead, extending for about two miles. These consisted of massive sarcophagi bearing deeply-incised inscriptions and sculptured scenes such as the one of Julia Velva now preserved in the Yorkshire Museum. She is shown reclining in bed while members of her family stand or are seated at the head and foot of the couch on either side of a three-legged table.

Most of the larger detached villas here are the result of development around 1833 and one of them, Number 125, — now joined with number 123 to make The Ambassador Hotel — was occupied for a time by William Gray (1815-83) secretary of the York and North Midland Railway Company.

On your right at the corner of Love Lane is the Elm Bank Hotel which was originally built about 1870 as a house for mill owner Sidney Leetham. It boasts the famous Walton Bar, designed in 1897 by George Walton and regarded by Sir John Betjeman as the best art nouveau interior in England.

Dropping down Mount Vale you pass on the right St Aubyn's Place which once was Seggy or Marsh Close and older houses now stand on adjacent land formerly called Fishermonger Close, sold by the city in 1837. Almost opposite is Newington Place — three houses built in 1823-7 which have now become a hotel. You are now rewarded on your left with a panoramic view of the Knavesmire race-course which became the venue for the 'sport of kings' in 1731.

Tyburn stone.

Climbing gently within a few yards you reach on your left the site of the dreaded Tyburn gallows (popularly known as the 'three-legged mare') where an inscribed stone on a raised area of seating commemorates the Catholic martyrs who died here for their faith.

On 1 March 1379 York Tyburn was established. It was a cold, blustery day when a special meeting was held at York Castle. The Mayor of the city, Mr John de Acaster, met with the bailiffs and other members of the Grand Jury to select a place to erect a new gallows.

York was well endowed with facilities for the execution of criminals. The Archbishop had a scaffold which stood in the Horsefair near the present junction of Haxby and Wiggington Roads. The Abbot of St Mary's possessed a gallows in Burton Stone Lane and the gallows of St Leonard's Hospital was near Garrow Hill.

After much discussion it was agreed that the gallows be erected on the Knavesmire at the side of the road to Tadcaster about a mile from the castle.

On the Wednesday morning of 9 March 1379 the new gallows was erected and became known as York Tyburn after the London gallows erected in 1196 and named after the stream called the Ty which flowed into the Thames.

In 1537 a new type of criminal was executed here. These were the Catholics who refused to accept the Act of Supremacy of 1534 which made it high treason to refuse to acknowledge Henry VIII as Supreme Head of the Church of England.

When Elizabeth came to the throne in 1558 a new wave of persecution swept over the Catholic Church and it was during this period that Blessed Margaret Clitherow, the wife of a prosperous butcher who lived in the Shambles made this hallowed spot the place where she recited her night prayers. She persuaded the watchman at Micklegate Bar to help her when she managed to slip out from the gate, along Blossom Street, and down Mount Vale to the Tyburn. Her punishment was to be crushed to death on 25 March 1586 at Ouse Bridge.

In 1679 The Venerable Nicholas Postgate who said Mass all his life at Egton near Whitby was hanged, drawn and quartered at the age of 82. In the following year, Blessed Thomas Twing, a secular priest born at Heworth Hall was also hanged, drawn and quartered at York Tyburn. He was the last of the York Martyrs.

Numerous other people — some famous, some notorious like Dick Turpin — were executed here but probably one of the most remarkable incidents is recorded in *Drunken Barnaby's Itinerary*:

Here a piper apprehended
Was found guilty and suspended.
Being led to fatal gallows,
Boys did cry, 'Where is they bellows?
Ever must thou cease thy tuning!'
Answered he,' For all your cunning,
You may fail in your prediction.'
Which did happen without fiction.
For cut down and quick interred,
Earth rejected what was buried:
Half alive, or dead, he rises,
Gets a pardon next assizes,
And in York continues blowing,
Yet a sense of goodness showing.

Apparently in 1634 musician John Bartendale was executed here for some felony and after hanging three-quarters of an hour was cut down and buried near the gallows. A short time afterwards one of the local nobility from Haslewood Castle was riding past and thought he saw the earth move. He and his servant alighted and exhumed the buried, but not dead, piper who was taken back to the castle, afterwards being reprieved and later pardoned.

Cross the road, and just past Pulleyn Drive is the entrance to Hob Moor through a gateway in a white iron fence that has rose bushes and a privet hedge behind it. Go through the gateway and follow the path until you reach a fork where you keep to the right.

Just by the fork is the Hob Moor Stone which may have originated as a sixteenth century plague stone where money for payment of goods was placed in vinegar which was believed to be a disinfectant and preventive against the spread of the virulent disease. In 1604, when York was visited by one of the many plagues, the infected were housed in booths on Hob Moor and it is estimated that 3,512 died.

Hob Moor stone.

A vertical stone erected here by the freemen in 1717 is said to have been a sculptured figure of a Knight Templar of the Roos family of Ingman-thorpe near Wetherby. They were patrons of St Martin's church, Micklegate and may have held manorial rights over land hereabouts. The statue was placed on a pedestal bearing the inscription:

This statue long Hob's name has bore,
Who was a knight in times of yore,
And gave this common to the pore.

Hob is a diminutive of Robert which was a favourite Christian name of that branch of the Roos living at Ingmanthorpe.

Pass under a bridge carrying the East Coast main line of British Rail and over Holgate Beck to follow the path across the wide expanse of grass common formerly called Yorkys Moor. As you cross the moor bear slightly to the right towards the corner of the blue railings surrounding a school. Traverse the stile and proceed along the path between the railings and Holgate Beck on your right. At the entrance to the school bear right and cross the beck into Green Lane.

Holgate Mill.

Continue up Green Lane to the roundabout where you turn right along Hamilton Drive for about a quarter of a mile. Look to your left for the large green iron gates that mark the entrance to West Bank Park. The *Yorkshire Evening Press* of 22 July 1938, announcing the opening, said the park was "delightful in setting and design and contained many novel features in layout". Inside is a statue of Queen Victoria sculptured by G. M. Milburn who was commissioned with money raised by public subscription. Milburn had dozens of photographs and pictures of Queen Victoria which he studied as he worked on the statue. They were almost all front face and, needing profile views, Milburn finally used his wife as a model.

Proceed across the park, cutting through the rose gardens and surmounting a slight incline you will see the dominating tower of Holgate Mill.

When you reach the park exit on Acomb Road turn right and go downhill for about a hundred yards to a bus stop on the opposite side of the road. This marks the entrance of the narrow passageway up which you proceed and which brings you out immediately opposite the windmill — still an imposing structure despite its lack of sails.

There has been a mill on this site since the twelfth century and this is the last remaining one from a group of twenty which encircled York in the seventeenth century. The present structure was built by miller George

Waud (senior) between 1770 and 1792, producing both brown and white flour until the late 1920s. The mill's decline began about 1884 when York extended its boundaries and big housing estates were built on the former cornlands which had supplied the mill. It had the unusual feature of five sails but in 1924 they fell into partial disuse and by 1936 the last miller, Mr Thomas Mollett, had gone.

From this elevated position there is a good view of York Minster before you descend right into Windmill Rise and go down to join Poppleton Road where you cross and turn right.

A short way down you come to the junction with Acomb Road on your right. Off this road, along Lindley Street and Murray Street, is housing dating back to the 1880s.

Opposite is the Fox Inn, with a history going back to 1776, and an attractive carved sign set in the brickwork above the main entrance. Thomas Calvert opened an inn here in property which appears to have belonged to the manor of Acomb which was in the estate of the Archbishop of York and would explain why its sign was the Cross Keys of St Peter. Patronage must have been rather slim as Holgate was only a tiny hamlet with a population in 1823 of only eighty-three and a directory of the period was describing it as "a rural retreat". Various landlords had the pub until 1843 when for some unexplained reason the name changed to The Fox. As a commemorative stone above the entrance testifies, in 1878 a new, larger pub was built on the site and in 1899 it was acquired by Joshua Tetley & Son.

The Fox Inn, Acomb.

A few yards further on your right is the Collingwood Hotel, a late Georgian building once known as Holgate House. Plumber and glazier Edward Matterson became owner of the site and built the central part of the present structure together with stables, two gardens, outbuildings and a 'Garden House' about 1774 when the Manor of Acomb and Holdgate with Clifton was being enclosed. He either overstretched himself financially or built the property as a speculative venture and sold it to dealer John Iveson who soon went bankrupt, and by 1738 a George Dawson was the owner. As a serving officer in the Royal Navy he was summoned in 1785 to Portsmouth to command the frigate HMS *Phaeton* on a voyage to the Mediterranean so his wife Mary sold the house to Quaker philanthropist William Tuke. He bought it for fellow American Quaker, Lindley Murray, who had been advised on health grounds to secure a residence near York.

The American lawyer was soon to become famous for his *English Grammar* prepared at the request of the teachers in the Friends' Girls School and published in York in 1795. For over half a century it was the most useful and popular class-book in schools all over England and America, running to ninety-two editions. He lived here for thirty-nine years and wrote most of his famous Grammar in the Summer House (possibly the original Garden Room) of his garden which "was said to exceed in variety the Royal Garden at Kew". He laid at his own expense the first paving stones in Holgate Lane, provided a seat outside his home "for weary travellers" and died there aged eighty on 16 January 1826 and was interred in the Friends' Burial Ground on Bishophill.

Other occupants include the Backhouse family, proprietors of the famous Holgate Nurseries; Mr and Mrs W. W. Morrell who campaigned for the opening in 1891 of the city's first public library; and Mr D.L. Pressly, editor of the *Yorkshire Evening Press* for 18 years. By 1970 it was the headquarters building of the British Transport Police and in 1985 became the Collingwood Hotel.

Continue forward to pass on your left the entrance to the railway workshops. The first railway workshops in York were set up by the York and North Midland Railway Company in 1842. That was only three years after the railway had reached the city. Then, located in Queen Street, they occupied less than an acre and their main function was the repair of locomotives, carriages and wagons.

New wagon works were built in 1867 on a 17-acre site between Holgate Road and Leeman Road. The present carriage works, adjacent to the wagons works, opened in 1884. With the introduction of electric lighting for carriages, electrical and charging shops were added to the works in 1915.

During the First World War, the York works played an important part in the war effort, producing not only road and rail wagons but also tank carriers and water tank carts.

The main carriage building shop was destroyed by fire in December 1944 and twenty-one years later the works were modernised and reorganised at a cost of nearly £1 million.

Turn left up Wilton Rise and you will reach a flight of steps leading to a bridge over the railway sidings. From here there is an excellent view of the 'back door' of York station and the constant coming and going of trains. Once a maze of junctions, points, signals, and crossings leading to fifteen platforms, it was radically slimmed and the platforms cut to eleven in 1988 for electrification of the East Coast main line. At the same time as part of the £18 million scheme British Rail's most sophisticated solid state interlocking signalling system was installed.

Keep to the path — now called Cinder Lane — until it emerges on Leeman Road, once called Thief Lane. George Leeman, who gave his name to the road, was three times Lord Mayor, Member of Parliament in 1865, 1871 and 1874, as well as being chairman of the North Eastern Railway Company.

Continue under the "Marble Arch" which carries the railway lines north and east out of the city and keeping to your right you will join Station Road where a statue of George Leeman overlooks a colourful garden with a pond.

Statue of John Leeman

Almost unrecognised is Leeman's work as liberal councillor and alderman, particularly his concern for the sanitation of the city. He spent public money freely to improve York's appalling drains, and as a result achieved unwelcome notoriety for being the Lord Mayor when the city rate first hit two shillings in the pound. His funeral in 1882 was watched by an estimated 20,000 people. According to a *Yorkshire Evening Press* report, "His kindness, sympathy, and justice towards the working-classes, especially those employed on the railway, were proverbial".

The statue was paid for by public subscription started shortly after Leeman's death in 1882 and erected (not on its present site) some 35 years after Hudson's fall from favour, but it was *in situ* by January 1885 and unveiled by the Marquess of Ripon in the following April.

Some authorities have claimed that it was in reality that of George Hudson which the city put into cold storage when the Railway King fell from grace. Many years later it is said to have been brought out, dusted off, re-chiselled and turned into a likeness of George Leeman.

Turn right before crossing to the tree-shaded grass plot on the opposite side where about twenty gravestones are preserved of 185 victims of the cholera epidemic of 1832. This began with "a young man of intemperate habits" who lived in a court near Skeldergate ferry which was popularly known as "Hagworm's Nest Court". The newly appointed 'Board of Health' suggested burying the victims in the ramparts near Walmgate Bar but this was opposed by the Society of Friends. The next choice was land outside the walls between North Street Postern and Micklegate Bar. This also brought an outcry, particularly from the inhabitants of North Street, and there were riotous protests resulting in a burial being obstructed on 13 June. The Board replied by ordering all funerals to come by boat or alternatively along Micklegate whereupon all the residents of that street were up in arms. Visitors fled. Richer citizens closed their houses and shops. Trade suffered. But the Board of Health stuck to its guns and by the end of July the worst was over, although sporadic cases kept appearing. Not until 23 October did the *York Courant* feel able to say that it "had great satisfaction in announcing that by the blessing of God this city is wholly free from the pestilential disease with which it has been visited".

Opposite is the Royal York Hotel, formerly the Royal Station Hotel, which was designed by William Peachey and opened on 20 May 1878. It stands on the site of a Roman cemetery.

Through the hotel lounge runs part of an extensive corridor which extends from east to west along the full length of the building. Tradition says that local racehorse trainers used to make their jockeys run up and down the long corridor to lose weight, and while the lads puffed backwards and forwards the trainers gathered around the bar and waved them on.

Continue around to pass the railway station — one of the great buildings of Victorian England built 1873/7 (when it was then said to be the largest station in the world) to an original design by Thomas Prosser. Having cost about £400,000 with a most un-Victorian colour scheme of maroon, pale mauve, and white, it was opened on Sunday 25 June 1877.

Inside the main entrance in a bed of plants stands a nineteenth century North Eastern Railway semaphore signal, one of the last in use on a passenger line, which was taken out of service in 1984. Signals of this type, on former North Eastern Railway routes, were painted red until 1928 so it has been restored to its original condition and put on display as a memento of York's railway heritage.

The 800 feet long curved train shed with its radiating ribbed roof on Corinthian columns was described by one disenchanted shareholder as "a very splendid monument to extravagance". Heraldic arms of former railway companies can be seen in the spandrels of the roof supports behind the bookstall.

On the waiting room of Platform 8 is a bronze plaque to a York railman who gave his life to help others on the night the station was bombed in 1942. The man was station foreman William Milner who is shown against a background of scenes of the air raid.

The first bombs began to drop shortly after the 10.15 pm King's Cross to Edinburgh sleeper train rolled to a halt on Platform 4, and staff tried to help injured passengers.

Mr Milner of Fifth Avenue, Heworth was a keen member of the London and North Eastern Railway Ambulance (First Aid) Movement. Further supplies of first-aid equipment were needed to treat a woman passenger cut by glass — and the only source was in a building containing the lamp room which was already ablaze. Mr Milner went in to fetch the black tin "ambulance box" despite warnings that the building might collapse. It did and he never came out. He was posthumously awarded the King's Commendation for Gallantry.

Climb the gentle slope of Queen Street.

An earlier station described as being "at the end of Queen Street, without Micklegate Bar" existed behind the city walls on your left and this served passengers at the opening of the York and North Midland Railway in May 1839. Within two years this embryo station — in reality an open shed supported on iron pillars, a two-roomed shack and a small engine house — was replaced by an advanced design by York architect G.T. Andrews and this opened on 4 January 1841. This was the station used by a rather disgruntled Queen Victoria when she visited briefly with Prince Albert and five of her children on 13 September 1854, and it was also used by Charles Dickens when he visited his brother in the city or came to give his famous readings. It was demolished in 1966.

A contract worth £13,867.19s.9d for the first section of the link westwards

to Leeds and Selby was given in March 1837 to Crawshaw & Rush of
Dewsbury. This was for a track of 3 miles 20 chains and two expensive
bridges, one at Holgate and the other "on the York and London turnpike
near the third milestone".

The first trial trip was made on 6 April 1839 — to Copmanthorpe and
back — which took the then reasonable time of forty minutes. On 29 May
the York and North Midland line was formally opened when four hundred passengers, including a considerable number of women, were
packed into nineteen carriages drawn by two engines.

Eulogistically the *Yorkshire Gazette* reported:

*"All was speedily ready for the start, of which a preliminary
notice was given by the ringing of the bell and at the moment
of creeping into motion by the piercing whistle of each engine.*

*The huge, snake-like body was then seen making way with
an imperceptibly accelerated speed and stealing away
under the broad arch of the Holdgate Lane Bridge, was soon
lost to the sight of the crowds who thronged the station, the
adjacent bar walls and the ramparts. ... while the gay travellers
experienced the exciting sensation of the gradually increasing
swiftness, till they were borne along with the speed of a
racehorse past the admiring spectators that still for many a mile
thronged both sides of the line".*

Only a few yards further, as you swing towards your left, brings you
back to Micklegate Bar.

9

Last of the Windmills
BARKER TOWER

Barker Tower — Scarborough Bridge — The Esplanade —
Clifton Ings — Rawcliffe Landings — Shipton Road —
St Giles Road — Skelton Village — The Green — Church Lane —
Shipton Road — Stripe Lane — Overton Ings —
Poppleton Reach — Clifton Ings — Clifton Bridge —
Riverside Walk — Scarborough Bridge — Barker Tower.

approx. 7 miles

NORTH STREET POSTERN TOWER was originally called Barker Tower, a name probably derived from the barkers who prepared oak bark for the nearby tanners' yards. Used as a watch-tower, it was also linked to Lendal or St Leonard's Tower on the opposite side of the river by a chain or boom in times of war. This also prevented people entering or leaving the city without paying the tolls on goods which had been imposed in the middle of the fourteenth century. The chains were sold in 1553 and so were not available on the last occasion when the city's defences were used in earnest during the Civil War which started in 1642. Here too, a ferry operated for centuries and it was often used by St Leonard's Hospital to transport inmates over the river. After Lendal Bridge was built in 1863 the tower became a mortuary and then a council store.

The wide arch and two side passages were built by the Great North of England Railway Company in 1840 for access to their coal wharfs. The original postern was a small square-headed doorway, sacrificed for the personal convenience of the Earl of Huntingdon, Lord President of the North during the reign of Queen Elizabeth I. He requested that North Street Postern be enlarged so that his 'great horse' might go through, and the Corporation complied.

Spanning the river alongside is Lendal Bridge which probably gets its name from the former staith or "lendyng" of St Leonard's Hospital which once stood nearby.

The Corporation discussed the idea of a bridge here for twenty-two years from 1838. In June 1857 some 600 citizens had petitioned the Corporation with a request that work should proceed on the proposed bridge as the lack of one caused considerable inconvenience in getting to the railway

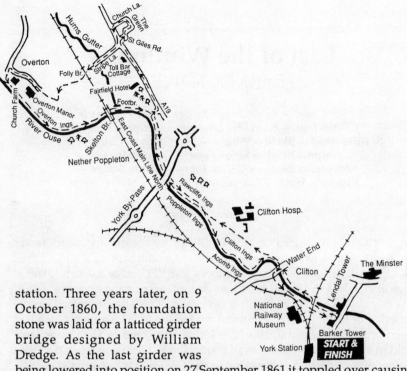

station. Three years later, on 9 October 1860, the foundation stone was laid for a latticed girder bridge designed by William Dredge. As the last girder was being lowered into position on 27 September 1861 it toppled over causing the whole structure to collapse into the river, killing five workmen and bringing construction to an abrupt end.

The present cast iron structure designed by Thomas Page, engineer of Westminster Bridge, was opened on 8 January 1863 to replace a ferry run by John Leeman since 1851. Four months later he was compensated for his loss of business with £15 together with a horse and cart. To celebrate the opening the Lord Mayor entertained 120 guests at the Mansion House, while the men who had worked on the structure sat down to their dinner in the "outer wool shed" adjoining the cattle market. Until 7 August 1894 a toll was payable and the old toll houses still remain.

Displayed on the bridge is the city coat of arms described heraldically as "argent, on a cross gules five lions guardant or". Historian Francis Drake in 1736 produced a romantic but factually dubious explanation for the choice of subject. He suggests that the arms were originally the cross of St George, but William the Conqueror, having been opposed during his siege of the city by a defence led by Sir Robert Clifford and four magistrates — Howngate, Talbot, Lassells, and Erringham — added the five lions "passant guardant or" in memory of the five defenders. As they are composed of the symbols of the patron Saint and the monarchy, the arms show the importance of the city in the kingdom and they were probably adopted between 1348 and 1370 during the reign of Edward II.

Next to the initials of Victoria and Albert are the cross keys of St Peter surmounted by the archbishop's crown, signifying the diocese of York, which were adopted by Robert Holgate in 1545 to replace an earlier version which can be seen on the West face of the gateway at Bishopthorpe Palace.

Decorating the balustrade is the white rose of York interspersed with the three lions of England

The City Crest on Lendal Bridge.

and the arms of the diocese, whilst in the centre an angel, based on Princess Alexandra of Denmark, supports the shield of St George.

Descend from the roadway down the little flight of steps and walk forward along the river bank to Scarborough Bridge built in 1844 to carry the York and Scarborough railway across the river, and from which it derives its name. Although primarily a railway bridge, from its first erection it also served as a footway. At first, this footway was in the middle between the up and down lines but in 1874 a section about eight feet wide was constructed on the south side at a lower level than the railway portion, especially for pedestrian traffic which it still serves.

The first bridge here was put up by Charles I on 7 September 1640 when he camped his army on either side of the river. The crossing then was a temporary structure supported by boats and taken away when the army left.

In 1877 a Roman coffin was found close by and from the inscription we know it belonged to Julia Fortunata, the Sardinian wife of Marcus Verecundias Diogenes, a wine merchant from the Bourges region of France.

Cross and descend to the Esplanade where you head up river away from the city. In July the verges are full of meadowsweet — foamy cream blossoms with a heady scent reminiscent of elder-flowers. Known also as "Queen of the Meadows" and "Maid of the Mead" it was once used for sweetening mead and the blossom is said to have the same properties as aspirin. According to seventeenth century herbalist Gerard, "the smell thereof makes the heart merrie, delighteth the senses: neither doth it cause Headache, or loathsomenesse to meat, as some other sweet-smelling herbes do". And in the days before carpets, meadowsweet leaves were a favourite to cover the floor and we are told Queen Elizabeth I "did more desire (them) than any other sweet herb to strew her chambers"

On your right are the playing fields of St Peter's School, the origins of which can be traced back to AD627 when Paulinus founded a teaching establishment here. Amongst the school's pupils was Tempest Anderson. Born in 1840 in Stonegate he devoted much time to the study of volcanoes and seismic phenomena, writing a book on the subject entitled *Volcanic Studies*. He travelled widely as a representative of the Royal Society and never returned from an expedition in 1912 after suffering an attack of enteric fever whilst in the area of the Red Sea. Dr Anderson was for many years the guiding spirit in the Yorkshire Philosophical Society and Tempest Anderson Hall in Museum Gardens was paid for out of money left to him in his sister's will.

St Peter's School

Before going under Clifton Bridge you can see marks recording the inundations of the river, one of the worst being in December 1978 when it was calculated that heavy rainfall deposited some 200 million tonnes of water on the River Ouse catchment area above York. An average flood brings the river up about 10 feet above summer level but the worst in recent times was 16ft 7ins (5.05m) in 1982 — not as bad as in 1947 at 17ft (5.18m) or 1632 with 17ft 6ins (5.33m); and in 1625 the waters reached 18ft 3ins(5.56m)!

Spread out ahead is Clifton Ings which in summer is a kaleidoscope of colour from a profusion of wild flowers casting off clouds of fragrance, whilst in winter it is submerged by about 2,300,000 cubic metres of flood waters to reduce the risks of flooding downstream.

Horse racing at York appears to have existed from the earliest days and Clifton Ings is claimed as the earliest battleground. There is a record in York City Corporation minutes of 9 April 1530 which gives conclusive evidence that York races had then been established for some time. The record runs:

"Whereas the ronnynge day of horsys between William Mallory Esq and Oswald Wyllesthorpe esquyer, was the Tuesday after Saynt George day, the xxijth yere of the reign of King Henry viijth, at the City of York. Yt upon it was concludyed & agreed by both the said gentylmen after ye forsaid Oswald hadde won the silver bell, before the right worshipful Robert Whitfield, alderman & lieutennant of the said City, of which day and place the said Oswald having the said bell delivered by the said lieutennant to his custody, promysed the said lieutennant to brying the said bell yt day xii mownthes and to deliver yt to the maior for yt tyme beyng, and also to bring with him yt same day a horse to run other for ye aforesaid bell, and also a wagon (? wager) of: viz Viijd, or more money as they can agree".

Camden in his *Britannia* published in 1586 tells us that "the Forest of Galtres is famous for a yearly horse-race, when the prize for the horse that wins is a little golden bell. It is hardly credible how great a resort of people there is to these races from all parts, and what great wagers are laid".

And in 1709 a certain Richard Tennant recorded on 21 September: "Was ye first time 4 mile heats were run for in Clifton Ings, Sir William Robinson making a large stone bridge, 9 yds broad, between Rockliffe & Clifton Ings at his own proper charge. There was a starting & a weighing-stoop at this end, &, at an equal distance, stoops to ye turns, & stoops at ye far end all painted white".

Follow the path directly across the Ings, as the river makes a broad loop to the left, before rejoining the path which then passes over a footbridge spanning a drainage dyke. Rawcliffe Ings ahead is united to Poppleton Ings on the opposite bank by the bridge carrying the £16 million ten-mile long outer bypass road carrying the A1237. Rawcliffe Bridge, opened on 11 December 1987, has six spans finished in textured concrete on precast concrete piles. This 178 metres long reinforced concrete bridge, which took nine months to build, is one of four in the central one-mile section of the bypass which received more than 20,000 tonnes of ballast from Rampton in Nottinghamshire via the Rivers Trent, Humber, and Ouse in a fleet of six barges each with a capacity of 300 tonnes.

After passing a small copse with manicured grass which appears to be the front lawn of a bungalow, you are at Rawcliffe Landings. Go through a metal gate in the hedge and turn immediate right around the side of the bungalow to go up a track past a terrace of three houses with five chimneys to emerge on the main road (A19) where you cross and turn left. The road crosses a beck called Burtree Dam before a milestone which tells travellers that they are 3 miles from York, 10 Miles from Easingwold and 199 miles from London. This marks the spot where, in turnpike days, those wishing to avoid the toll-gate ahead would turn off by a field track to go round by Skelton landing.

Opposite is Fairfield Manor Hotel.

An old deed of 1815 states that the elegant Georgian mansion 'Fair Field' was built by John Kilby prior to that date — probably about 1805 — but by 1818 it was owned by George Vanderpant Drewry. He obtained a mortgage from Richard John and Henry Thompson who in 1832 took possession. Henry Thompson lived here until 1864 when he sold the property to a prize fighter called John Jackson who held it until his death in 1870 and ran the place as a stud-farm.

Neighbouring land and riverside Ings had long been in the hands of descendants of Sir William Robinson and from him passed to the de Greys. In 1874 Earl de Grey bought Fairfield estate for £15,500. His kinsman, Captain Robert de Grey Vyner was soon breeding here some of the most famous horses in English racing, using the old Clifton Ings course as a training ground. These included *Lambkin*, winner of the 1884 St Leger, and *Minting* which took the Jubilee Cup at Ascot in 1887.

The mansion was well supplied with the comforts of the day. A private gasworks in the grounds supplied the illuminations at a time when this was advanced technology; a private laundry was installed to deal with the starched linen of the elite who visited. The elaborate oak panelling on the staircase and in the reception area reflects the same styles found at Newby and Beningborough Halls, while the mirror at the foot of the stairs was designed for costumes of a vanished elegance.

A frequent visitor in those palmy days was the then Prince of Wales, later King Edward VII, who found distraction at the card-tables and in the billiards room. At the turn of the century the house passed into the hands of the Countess of Rosslyn, a determined lady with advanced views who was one of the first in the district to own a motor-car.

The royal connection was continued, and when Princess May of Teck, the future Queen Mary, became engaged to the Duke of Connaught, she came to stay at Fairfield and the occasion was celebrated by the construction of a new front entrance, now part of the reception complex.

In 1911 York Corporation bought the house and adapted it as a hospital for treating patients with tuberculosis and in 1923 added a children's ward and school.

It was converted into a 25-bedroomed hotel and restaurant in September 1980.

Toll Bar Cottage, a little further along on the left — set back on a bit of the old road — is a reminder of the imposts collected here, for this was the York-Easingwold-Thirsk Turnpike from 1752 until 1875 when it became toll-free. A late eighteenth century document tells how hawkers used to evade the toll bar by taking the road down to Skelton landing which used to branch off the main road at the boundary line near Fairfield. They

Toll Bar Cottage.

would then go across the fields and up the road from Overton to rejoin the main road. The practice was stopped when the landowner blocked the road down to the landing, but this inconvenienced genuine travellers and the document is a case made by twelve local worthies that it was a right of way from time immemorial.

Doubtless many a traveller got astride his steed with the aid of the mounting stone outside the Blacksmiths Arms which marks the point

The Blacksmiths Arm and mounting stone.

where you turn right up the rise towards the village of Skelton. This was formerly Smethybalke — the smith's fields — and it was a smithy's croft in 1807, with a working smithy operating here beyond the turn of this century. Although the house dates from the eighteenth century, it seems to have been the site of a smithy and possibly an ale-house back in 1630 and beyond.

The elevation of Skelton probably accounts for its name since the Anglo-Saxon 'scelf' means high ground and 'ton' is a settlement. The hillock overlooks the crossroads where the Roman highway from York to the North intersects with the minor route from Overton on the edge of the former Forest of Galtres. As Drayton puts it:

When that great forest nymph,
fair Gautress on her way
She seems to stand prepared
with garland fresh and gay
To deck up Ouse, before herself
to York, she show.

In medieval times Skelton was under the control of the King's Forester who administered the complex forest laws. Existing villages, for example, were not allowed to expand their boundaries without permission, and foresters had the unpopular task of enforcing this by prosecuting anyone who "assarted", that is grubbed up trees in order to cultivate more land. In addition to such crimes as poaching it was an offence to cut peat, take out loads of wood, and unlicensed feeding of sheep. Herds of sheep passing through the forest were charged a toll of twelve pence for each hundred.

Walk forward up St Giles Road which bears left and turn right up The Village past the General Store and Post Office to arrive at The Green where you turn left.

Ahead, overlooking the tiny green and almost hidden by huge trees, is the village pride — the most perfect thirteenth century parish church in England, not only for its design and craftsmanship but also on account of its near-miraculous completeness. St Giles' church was a source of inspiration to the architects of the nineteenth century Gothic Revival.

St Giles Church, Skelton.

The reason for such an architectural gem being in a small village like Skelton can be traced back to 1247 when Roger Haget, Treasurer of York Minster, provided an annuity of twenty pence for the first known priest here, Robert of Leeds. Whether Haget built the church is not recorded but the fabric does bear mute testimony to the fact that the construction was the work of masons responsible for the transepts of York Minster, and the task was carried out as a single project around 1240. Perhaps it was this general similarity to the Minster that prompted the theory first mooted in 1731 by Thomas Gent, that the church was made with materials left over from the building of the Minster transepts.

A remarkably sympathetic restoration was carried out between 1814 and 1818 by Henry Graham, son of the rector of St Saviour's, York. By 1846 the village was on the itinerary of every serious student of medieval architecture after a young architect called Ewan Christian published *Architectural Illustrations of Skelton Church, Yorkshire*. The almost inevitable sequel occurred in 1883 when he carried out a second restoration.

With its steep roof and fine twin-arched bellcote it appears quite majestic yet it covers an area of only 55 by 42 feet overall and is capable of fitting easily into the central aisle of either transept of York Minster. The external walls of the church are constructed entirely from magnesian limestone ashlar of a quality normally found only in the great medieval churches. On the apex of the east gable is one of the finest of the few thirteenth century gable crosses to have survived anywhere, but the south door is the showpiece of the exterior although it has become extremely dilapidated over the years since it was entirely renewed in 1811 by Michael Taylor, a stonemason whose uncannily skilful copying of Gothic detail can be seen on the lower part of York Minster's west front.

Inside, almost every stone has scratched upon it a mason's mark and nearly all the same marks occur on the stones of the York Minster transepts if confirmation of the association is needed.

On the east wall of the north chapel (now the vestry) is a tablet to Joseph and Sarah Hotham erected in 1791 by their son Sir Richard Hotham, a wealthy hatter of Southwark, London and founder of Bognor Regis, the first sea-bathing resort.

Just a couple of centuries ago Bognor Regis was just a fishing and smuggling hamlet in the Sussex parish of South Bersted. But on 18 January 1787 the vicar noted in his parish register that the foundation stone of a "public bathing place" was laid by Sir Richard Hotham. This was the start of Bognor Regis as the first resort in Britain to be specially built for sea bathing. The new Bognor took shape in 1789/90 with a hotel, terraces of houses, stabling, assembly rooms, mansions, and a special house for George II if he wished to visit the town.

Hotham's efforts to have the town named Hothampton were unsuccessful, although the town does have a Hotham Bowling Club and Hotham Park.

Provision of the memorial to his parents at Skelton is the only recorded connection with the village, despite considerable detailed research by various people over many years. Hotham's birthplace too remains a blank

— it could have been Skelton — but at least it is certain that he was born on 5 October 1722. This was confirmed in a rather macabre way by the lead coffin plate which fell off when his remains were re-interred in 1879. A "William Hotham of York" was mentioned in Sir Richard's will and a Hotham said to have been connected with him was "in a cloth manufactory in Leeds, near the Town Hall", according to a record of 1898.

In addition to its architectural attractions, the church boasts a graveyard which contains a wealth of wildlife. Blackbirds, robins, greenfinches, chaffinches, starlings, mistle thrush, tawny owl, willow warbler, and spotted flycatcher are just a few of the birds which find feeding areas, roosting and nesting sites amongst the surrounding tall trees as well as newly planted horse chestnut and silver birch. A good concentration of insect life provides nourishment for bats and shrews which keep company with the bank vole amongst the lichen-covered gravestones and the diversity of wild flowers including the greater celandine.

Various gravestones feature poetic memorials beloved of our Victorian ancestors, but the true story behind the inscription to Edward Walters who died on 3 April 1780 awaits discovery. This reads:

> *Great was his genius*
> *But small his conduct*
> *Courteous Reader*
> *Step softly over the grave*
> *Of this unfortunate young man.*

After visiting the church turn left down Church Lane to reach the main road again.

Unfortunate were the monks encountered hereabouts by a Norman army, according to Francis Drake in his *Eboracum* published in 1736. He recounts:

> *"William the Conqueror, in the third year of his reign (on St Thomas's day) laid siege to the city of York, but finding himself unable, either by policy of strength, to gain it, raised the siege; which he had no sooner done, but by an accident he met with two fryers at a place called Skelton, not far from York, who, being examined, told him they belonged to a poor fryery of St Peter's in York and had been to seek reliefs for their fellows and themselves against Christmas; the one having a wallett full of victualls and a shoulder of mutton in his hand, with two great cakes hanging round his neck; the other having bottles of al, with provisions likewise of beife and mutton in his wallett."*

William gave them money and a promise to build a priory endowed with large revenues and privileges if they would let him and his army into the

Old cross, Overton.

city at an agreed time. They agreed and that night the Normans entered and took the city. The result was St Peter's which later became St Leonard's.

Drake goes on to claim that each year on St Thomas's Day the city compelled a friar from the monastery to undergo a vicious form of penance for their ancestor's treachery. He was dragged behind a horse paraded through the streets of York.

Turn left and walk back to the Blacksmiths Arms before crossing to go down Stripe Lane signposted to Overton. After going over Hurns Gutter the lane goes under the East Coast main line of British Rail and takes a zigzag course over the fields to enter Overton where the remains of an old cross can be seen on the left. The hamlet is almost as remote now as when the Abbot of St Mary's had his country residence here. All that remains are parts of the moat, for the building was demolished in 1736 and some of its stones were incorporated into a farmhouse. Indeed little is known about the establishment apart from the visit of an antiquary in 1661 who recorded a Latin inscription carved on a beam stating the house was built *Anno Dom MCCCCCVI et regni regis Henri Septimi*. Church Farm, Church Lodge tell of these ecclesiastical associations and Vicarage House boasts an unusual weathervane of two flying geese.

Their are distant views across the fields to the White Horse on the Hambleton Hills as you proceed to Church Farm where the lane swings sharp right. Turn left down the path bearing the York Amalgamation of Anglers sign on the fence and go over a stile to reach the bank of the River Ouse where you turn left to follow the wide sweep around Overton Ings.

As you near Nether Poppleton on the opposite bank you can see an unusual peace memorial of a rocky cairn strewn with flowers and commemorating twelve villagers who gave their lives in two World Wars. Further along a colourful board indicates the landing stage for the Fox Inn reached by a worn path up the steeply sloping grass. A four-hundred-year-old farmhouse before it was turned into an inn about 1906, the Fox Inn

Sloop turning in the River Ouse.

was extended and modernised in 1970 to cater for the burgeoning river trade.

Continue along Poppleton Reach to pass under the railway line again once the setting for the famous steam-hauled "Railway Races to the North" marking the intense competition between the railway companies operating the East and West Coast routes. High speed electric locomotives now thunder across the River Ouse where in 1888 the steam-hauled London to Edinburgh express that became the *Flying Scotsman* was vainly covering the 393 miles in nine hours.

A footbridge crosses Hurns Gutter as it feeds into the river which makes a broad sweep past Rawcliffe Landings as you retrace your steps back towards the city. At Clifton Ings keep to the right along the towpath of the river as it skirts Acomb Ings on the opposite bank.

Dominating the skyline are the silos and chimney of the sugar beet factory built nearby in 1926 which handles more than 500,000 tonnes of beet a year. In the 1978/8 season sugar beet from 1,200 local farmers was used to produce a daily average of 830 tonnes of sugar and 450 tonnes of animal feed.

The path follows the river as it bends away from the waterworks whose tale is told in a survey of Acomb included in Bulmer's *North Yorkshire* printed in 1890.

"In the year 1682 during the reign of Charles II, waterworks were first established in the Sendal (Lendal) Tower in York. A pumping engine, worked by two horses, was placed in the tower by means of which a scanty supply of water was furnished the citizens every week.

The mains at that time were the trunks of trees hollowed out and fastened together and laid down in the streets. This went on for nearly a century when the works were purchased by Col. Thornton who made considerable improvements in the service of the water. At his death, a steam engine was introduced by his son who enlarged the building and introduced hot and cold baths in a house adjoining the tower.

In 1799, another company was formed, the tower was raised and iron mains substituted for wooden pipes. At this time, one half of the people got water Mondays, Wednesdays and Fridays and the other half, Tuesdays, Thursdays, and Saturdays, for two hours only and then the water was just as it came from the river.

In 1846 a new company was formed and secured a site at Acomb Landing a few yards higher up than Clifton Scope on which they erected a commodious building and placed in it two powerful steam engines for pumping water from the river".

The book also gives an indication how York has grown since 1880. "The present consumption of water amounts to over 2,200,000 gallons daily" it says. Nowadays, the city uses over 11m gallons a day. Over 173,000 customers in 130 square miles around the city including parts of Rydale, Selby, and Harrogate are served by York Waterworks Company.

Past Clifton Bridge bear left up the slope and left again to cross the bridge. Descend immediately by the steps to the riverside path which crosses a grassy sward before going under a line of weeping willows to join a combined cycleway and footpath from the right where you are faced by the bulk of the National Railway Museum housed in the former steam-engine shed which was a cathedral for railway-lovers.

Here is displayed the finest and largest collection of material relating to the history and development of the British Railway system in the world. Opened by HRH the Duke of Edinburgh on 27 September 1975 — an especially appropriate choice in view of the royal rolling-stock preserved here — it boasts an outstanding collection of steam, diesel and electric locomotives, carriages and freight wagons. audio visual programmes, vehicles, signalling, uniforms, tickets, memorabilia, models, posters, pictures, and even railway music, showing the great changes brought by the railways. Probably one of the most significant exhibits is Sir Nigel Gresley's famous 4-6-2 Class A4 locomotive *Mallard*. In its striking blue livery, number 4468 is a perpetual reminder of the zenith of steam traction on the railways of this country for on 3 July 1938 *Mallard* reached 126 mph descending Stoke Bank to create a world speed record for steam locomotives.

Follow the pathway back to Scarborough Bridge to retrace your steps for the final few yards back to North Street Postern.

10

Mother of Jorvik
LENDAL TOWER

Lendal Tower — The Esplanade — Marygate — Marygate Lane —
Clifton Green — Water End — Water lane — Lumley Street —
Burton Stone Lane — Grosvenor Road — Bridge Lane —
Clarence Street — Gillygate — Bootham — Marygate —
Museum Gardens — Lendal Tower.

approx. 2½ miles

STANDING SENTINEL at the north end of Lendal Bridge is Lendal Tower, originally St Leonard's Tower taking its name from St Leonard's Landing below the great medieval hospital.

This great hospital, which covered a vast area on the north bank of the River Ouse, was founded and endowed by King Athelstan in AD936 and was at first dedicated to St Peter. Some extent of its activities can be gained from a record of 1293 which tells that its infirmary had accommodation for 229 men and women patients whilst an adjoining orphanage housed twenty-three boys; 232 loaves and 256 herrings were given away every week at its gate; thirty-three dinners and fourteen gallons of beer were distributed every Sunday, together with dinners for eight lepers. In addition to these gifts, every Sunday each prisoner in the Castle, numbering at that time 310, received a small loaf. This service for the sick and poor was carried on for more than six hundred years.

The tower provides an unusual headquarters for York Waterworks Company — one of the oldest in the country. On 1 April 1677 a lease was granted by the Mayor and Commonalty to an enterprising London merchant, "for encouraginge and enablinge the said Henry Whistler to erect and make a waterhouse and waterworks for the service and accomendac'on of the inhabitants of the said City of Yorke". This runs for five hundred years at a rent "of one Pepper Corne on the feast day of All Saints in every yeare (if itt be lawfully demanded) and noe more". At the outset the water was simply pumped into supply pipes made from bored-out tree trunks. A Newcomen steam engine was installed in the mid-eighteenth century and rebuilt in 1781 and 1784 by John Smeaton. This worked until 1849 when the new York Waterworks Company moved the waterworks to Acomb Landing.

Descend the steps from the bridge down to the river bank in front of the

Kingsway · Shipton Rd. · Water La. · Lumley Rd. · Water End · Health Centre · Burton Stone Lane · York City F.C. · York Dist. Hosp. · Wigginton Rd. · Haxby Rd. · Bridge La. · The Avenue · Clifton Br. · Grosvenor Rd. · Bootham Cres. · Bootham Park Hosp. · Lowther St. · Clarence · Clifton · River Ouse · The Esplanade · Qu. Anne Sch. · Bootham · Gillygate · Lord Mayor's Walk · Marygate · Abbey · Bootham Tower · The Minster · Museum Gdns · Museum · Scarborough Br. · Lendal Tower · Lendal Br. · York Station · **START & FINISH**

tower. There was for many years a ferry service here, leased by the Corporation to the highest bidder. But in July 1524 the authorities were having to temper commerce with compassion when they determined "that William Launcedayle, ferryman, shall pay for the common ferry this yeare but XI.s. farme*, considering that he is but a poore man and the profetts of the said ferry decayed." However in 1545 it had a ferrywoman in the shape of Jennet Collywood, but from 1850 it was John Leeman who plied the trade. In 1862, the last year of operation, Leeman carried some 293,460 passengers — over 800 a day.

Walk away from the bridge along The Esplanade which is a favourite mooring for pleasure cruisers. There was once a wall along the river front of St Mary's Abbey grounds, later known as the Manor Shore, but this has long since been destroyed. The river front was piled and the esplanade constructed in 1832. In 1844 the city arms were placed on the stone posts

---

*   a fixed payment, a lease

York Waterworks, Lendal Tower.

supporting the iron railings along the boundary of Museum Gardens.

The abbey was founded here in 1087 when Alan of Betagne, Earl of Richmond gave the church of St Olave and four acres of adjacent land to Stephen of Lastingham. In 1089 the foundation of the new church was laid and the dedication changed from St Olave to St Mary. The abbot of St Mary's had the honour of being mitred and had a seat in Parliament for which reason he had the title of Lord Abbot. He also had jurisdiction not only over the monastery but in the extensive district known as the liberty of St Mary where he held courts and sentenced to imprisonment or death. The abbot had several country houses, one of which was at Overton some three miles up river. His journeys there, with his grand and numerous retinue, were usually made in his state barge which he boarded at St Mary's Landing where stands the Water Tower.

Clifton Green.

This retains its arrow-slits and doorway but has lost its crenellated parapet since 1700. The tower was part of the protective walls which surrounded St Mary's Abbey founded in the shelter of an old fortification which had been the seat of the Saxon Earls of Northumbria and so was known as Earlsborough — a name retained by a terrace on the left.

Turn right and walk up Marygate — a street which frequently figured in disputes between the abbot of St Mary's and the city authorities — and shortly after passing the tile-hung half-timbered Bay Horse pub built in 1894 turn left into the narrow Marygate Lane. Notice the old gas lamp converted to electricity as you walk through the narrow passageway which opens out to pass Abbots Mews Hotel on your right. Ignore pointers to St Mary's Lane as you go forward alongside a wall whose base is probably stones from St Mary's Abbey. Proceed through the narrow snicket under the York to Scarborough railway line and across Bootham Terrace to pass Queen Anne's School on your left.

The path now skirts the cricket ground of St Peter's School, and, where it forks around an old oak tree, keep to the right to cross The Avenue and continue forward through a narrow passageway behind some houses. Ignore opportunities to turn right as you wind your way forward to exit at Clifton Green. Immediately on your left is No 16 — a curious little house with stained glass coats of arms in its windows.

Distinguished architect George Pace writing in 1956 said of this townscape:

"Clifton Green is a Victorian townscape of a high order. The green itself with its fine trees, its park-like grass (economically maintained by grazing horses), its white-painted rails and its water trough is perfect, except for the utterly unfeeling shelter and police-sub-station, which the present century has intruded. The surrounding flagged paths, cobbles and setts, the little Puginesque house with its elaborate vane, its mullioned windows, and coat of arms, the cottages, the array of vast houses and terraces, Clifton Church, all go to build up an urban scene of a high order, one which should be zealously guarded against the inroads of Subtopia. Whenever alteration to any given part is considered, the proposals should be given searching aesthetic scrutiny by one who really understands what is involved. Clifton Green may well be as much an object of pilgrimage 150 years hence as the Shambles are today!"

Cross the corner of the green by the little paved footway and turn right along Water End to follow the white fence towards the traffic lights.

Where the cattle trough now stands, a century ago there was a horsepond about sixty feet in diameter fed by Bur Dyke which flowed along the north side of Water Lane and was culverted under the turnpike road of the York and Northallerton Trust into the pond. It then flowed south west across the Green to form the boundary between the parishes of St Michael-le-Belfry to the north and St Olave in the south. Today the Bur Dyke sometimes backs up from the Ouse at flood times and forms impressive lakes as happened in March 1947, December 1978 and January 1982.

And Bur Dyke figures large in one of York's oldest traditions maintained at Clifton — the Manor of Clifton Court Leet. The court, one of only six in Yorkshire and of only thirty-eight in the country, dates from Anglo-Saxon times and meets each year on the second Wednesday of October to check the conditions of Clifton's ancient water courses. One of the court's tasks is to see whether Bur Dyke, mentioned in the Domesday Book, and other water courses are free of debris and if not to amerce (fine) those responsible for their maintenance. Bridges too are inspected by the Steward of the

Manor and his jurymen as part of the ritual and nominal fines imposed on offenders.

At the traffic lights cross Shipton Road (A19) ahead. This road has seen many important personages. In 1323 King Edward II in the course of his flight from the Scots who had vanquished his army at the Battle of Byland Abbey, six miles north of Easingwold, narrowly escaped capture as he fled through the Forest of Galtres. He found refuge in York where he stayed several months, diverting his chagrin at this defeat "with all the amusements he could encompass".

Queen Phillipa, the consort of King Edward III, gathered an army in York in 1346 to resist an invasion of England by David Bruce, King of Scotland and she marched at its head through here to Nevill's Cross and returned victorious the same way.

There came this way too a massive army under the leadership of Archbishop Scrope in the rebellion against King Henry IV in 1405. Scrope had preached a seditious sermon in York Minster whereupon 20,000 men joined his standard before marching out of the city through Bootham and encamping near the village of Shipton in Galtres Forest. Act IV Scene 1 of the second part of Shakespeare's play *Henry IV* is set here and simply described as "A Forest in Yorkshire"

At the corner to your right is Abbey Street at the north corner of which was reputed to stand the last of the Galtres Forest trees which was taken down in the summer of 1948.

Clifton formed a part of the large Forest of Galtres which spread north, east and west of York and covered thousands of acres; it covered the twenty miles between the city walls and Aldborough near Boroughbridge. According to a contemporary medieval description, "many places were thick and shady with lofty trees and underwood but others were wet flat boggy moorish quagmires — a dreary waste extending north".

Like all forests it was owned by the king of the moment. Galtres teemed with game like wild boar, hare, deer and animals like the fox and rabbit, as well as birds. It was a haven for poachers, and the king protected his rights by letting parts of the forest to local lords of the manor who were made responsible for enforcing the multitude of laws through the forest courts. For example, the penalty for hunting without permission was the loss of an eye. They were also required to ensure that the royal larder was always well stocked with venison and other fresh meat as well as selling animals seized from people who owed money to the king.

In 1281 Nicholas de Meynel was permitted to hunt foxes and hares with his own hounds and more than a century later Richard II allowed Ralph de Neville of Raskelf to enclose part of the wood and build a park.

And a record dated 1215 tells how King John ordered the bailiffs of Galtres Forest to "allow the mayor and citizens of York to have what is necessary from the woods in your bailiwick for fortifying the same our city."

In the fifteenth century, persons travelling northwards were usually accompanied through the Forest by armed guides who were stationed at Bootham Bar. After sunset a beacon fire in the beautiful lantern tower of All Saints Church, Pavement cast its light over the surrounding country to guide the travellers. After 1670 a great portion of the Forest was cleared and the land brought under cultivation.

Go forward to enter Water Lane where you pass on your right Freemens Court and Grosvenor Court before Pinfold Court. Bear sharp right here at the fork where Water Lane swings left and Kingsway is ahead, to go behind the health centre and beside Kingsway Junior School. When you reach some stone bollards on your right go through to walk down Lumley Street to Burton Stone Lane which was only a country lane until suburban residential development began about 1850.

Turn right along Burton Stone Lane — which derives its name from the plague stone preserved behind railings outside the Burton Stone Inn alongside the main road. At the northern end of Burton Stone Lane, to your left, stood the Abbot's gallows on which criminals convicted in the Abbot's court expiated their crimes. Some authorities suggest that a wooden gate called Galmanhawlith marked the entrance to the forested region beyond Burton Stone Lane and took its name from the gallows. This would mean 'Gate of Gallows Haw', that is 'the hedged enclosure in which the gallows stood'.

Hereabouts stood a windmill from the late fourteenth century which was offered for sale in 1807 and was still standing in 1852. On the 1819 marriage bond of William Clarkson, described as a miller of Clifton who operated Burton mill from 1843 to 1849, is the signature of Richard Chicken whom many consider to be the prototype for Charles Dickens' character Mr Micawber.

Ahead of you is Duncombe Barracks where you turn right to skirt Lumley Barracks with its ornate crest and 1911 date overhead. Here is the headquarters of 1st Battalion Yorkshire Volunteers (Cleveland) and the 2nd Battalion Yorkshire Volunteers (Yorkshire and Humberside).

Turn left almost immediately and proceed along Grosvenor Road. This is slightly north of the old Kenningdyke which once marked the boundary of land lying behind houses in Bootham. A statement of the city boundaries of 1374/5 includes mention of the fact that there was a right of common for all citizens in those crofts that lay beyond the Kenningdyke.

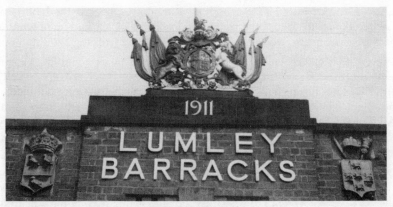

Lumley Barracks crest.

On your left you now pass the Bootham Crescent headquarters of York City Football Club where they first played in 1932. Founded in 1922, the club was elected to the Football League Division 3 North in 1929 but in 1959 they failed on goal average to retain that status and so became founder members of Division 4. Since then they have established themselves as a 'yo-yo' club — five times promoted, four times relegated and seven applications for re-election. Having only just avoided relegation in 1972/3 by winning their last game at Rotherham, the following season they finished third with 61 points and so gained promotion to Division 2 for the first time in their history. But by 1980/1 they were at the bottom of the Football League and so had to make their seventh application for re-election.

When you reach the junction of Scarborough Terrace and Grosvenor Terrace cross forward to climb the steps over the York to Scarborough railway line whose existence we owe to 'Railway King' George Hudson who raised funds for the project in 1843. The proposed route was to cross the Clifton property of important landowner Earl de Grey. Consequently when in January 1844 his manager John Bower received the usual notice of intent to purchase by the railway company he lost no time in informing the noble Earl. His letter of 24 February 1844 not only highlights the depreciation of the land "by cutting and mangling for upwards of a mile" but hints at the very nadir in the fortunes of the village of Clifton "by making of a station for coals, as Mr Hudson is a wholesale trader in railways and coals".

Meanwhile two local residents — John Russell, a solicitor and the Revd Danson Currer — consulted the plans and decided that the railway would run through the solicitor's garden and be uncomfortably close to the clergyman.

The Revd Currer took on the mantle of leader of the opposition to the railway, raising significant funds for the task and proving himself to be a consummate letter-writer to some twenty-two Members of Parliament. No less than fifty residences would be affected by the railway of which thirty were occupied by independent families including clergymen, esquires, widows, and officers in addition to three schools for young ladies, an Old Maids' hospital and the County Lunatic Asylum.

Writing from Clifton House on 13 March 1844, Danson Currer advised Earl de Grey that George Hudson's "emissaries had been getting up a counter petition to use which has merely been signed by a few of Your Lordship's tenants and others under his influence, some of whom do but act in obedience to his dictation, and one solicitor having the fear of Mr Hudson has withdrawn his name from our petition and also his subscription of £5".

After suffering defeat in the House of Commons, Danson Currer sought the support of the House of Lords in an endeavour to have the line diverted away from Clifton and success attended the first efforts of the Petitioners. But Earl de Grey seems to have been heartily sick of the wrangling and withdrew his support with the result that opposition collapsed. On 5 August 1844 Hudson announced that Royal Assent had been given to the York and Scarborough Railway Act "after an opposition as unjust and unfair as was ever offered in Parliament to a public improvement".

On 7 July 1845 two trains carrying directors and their friends made the first journey from York to Scarborough and back for a great dinner that same evening in the Guildhall. Locomotives *Hudson* and *Lion* hauled the trains next day when the line was opened to the public.

Proceed along Bridge Lane alongside the City Hospital whose children's ward windows are decorated with colourful cartoon characters.

At the junction with Wiggington Road and Haxby Road dominated by The Punch Bowl pub turn sharp right into Clarence Street which is part of the ancient highway to Helmsley and had no dwelling houses until about 1835.

At this junction now overlooked by the huge Wesleyan Chapel of 1883, there stood in medieval times a gruesome spectacle. For a century after the Norman Conquest the right to administer justice was commonly granted to influential individuals and corporations to enable them to keep the king's peace. Imprisonment as punishment was unknown although it often preceded trial; sentence on conviction usually consisting of branding, maiming, or hanging — usually hanging. Here stood the gallows of the Dean and Chapter of York Minster who had the rights of holding court and passing sentence within all their estates.

The land on the right for the entire length of Clarence Street was for centuries an open space of several acres which was called Horsefair. Three great fairs were held here every year. These fairs were anciently claimed to be the right of the Abbot of St Mary's — a claim which produced much bad blood between the abbey folk and the citizens — but on some unnamed occasion the Abbot relinquished his claim, the settlement vesting the tolls of two of the fairs in the Mayor and Commonalty of York and those of the third in the Archbishop.

When the two city fairs for the sale of horses and cattle were held the sheriffs of the city rode into the fair by way of Burton Stone Lane and back through Gillygate.

On the southern corner of Horsefair, a short way back from Clarence Street near the entrance to Union Terrace on your right stood the Hospital of Our Lady established by Robert Pykering who was Dean of the Minster 1312-1332, but it is thought that the building was in use many years earlier. An Inquisition was held in September 1314 in which these premises were described as "A Chapel of the Blessed Virgin Mary, where the Prior and Friars of the Order of the Blessed Mary of Mount Carmel used to live".

The principal purpose of this hospital was to provide a home for retired and disabled members of the Minster clergy before it was confiscated by the crown in 1547.

In 1555, two years after Queen Mary came to the throne, and whilst the Catholic regime was for a time fully re-established, the question of the education of potential priests was raised. Quick off the mark the Dean and Chapter of York Minster petitioned Queen Mary and her consort Philip in 1556 for use of St Mary's Hospital in the Horsefair. And on 14 March 1557 a licence was issued transferring the property. The grant states "Whereas the Dean and Chapter of the cathedral church of St Peter of York are minded and have intent to found and establish a Grammar School near their cathedral church . . . we give licence . . . to grant and confirm the said hospital to the Dean and Chapter . . . We grant that the school shall be called the Cathedral School of St Peter in York."

St Peter's School had its home here until 1644 when the building was pulled down by order of the royalist military commander to provide for the more effective defence of the city in the then impending siege. The school then had various homes before finally being transferred to Bootham in 1844 where it exists today.

One of its scholars — Robert Middleton born in York in 1570 — was beatified by the Pope in 1985. Although the England of the later sixteenth century was undergoing a fierce Protestant revival under the powerful leadership of Elizabeth I, there seems to have been a strong undercurrent of Roman Catholicism at St Peters.This is thought to have been due to the influence of headmaster John Pulleyn.

Middleton, who was possibly a relative of Margaret Clitherow, the York martyr who became a saint in 1970, espoused the Roman Catholic faith early on in life.After leaving school he worked as a clerk in London and Hull but at the age of 23 he decided to become a priest and sailed secretly to Calais. After nearly five years of study and a special blessing from the Pope he returned to England and was arrested in Ripon at Christmas 1599.

He was sentenced to be hanged, drawn and quartered at Lancaster. Such was his patience, holiness and cheerfulness that five other criminals were converted as Robert waited for his death.It is reported that he went "very nimbly" up the gallows in March 1601. According to the sentence he had to be cut down while still alive — but unconscious. After a while Robert was seen to move and the sheriff, as an act of mercy, ordered his head to be cut off before the rest of the sentence was carried out.

A manuscript in the British Museum has this epitaph for Robert Middleton:

Myld Middleton, oh what tongue
Can half thy vertue shewe.

Continue forward into Gillygate which in a document dated between 1145 and 1161 is referred to as *Via Sancti Egidii*. In 1330 it was called Sayngiligat but it is generally accepted that it owes its name to the church of St Giles which was declared redundant in 1547 and taken down. Nothing is known of its patronage or foundation and the parish was eventually united with St Olave's in 1585, but the churchyard remained in use for many years and in 1605 plague victims were buried there. By 1630 the site was privately owned by one George Blackallar. Macabre documents dated 1575 to 1698, record that "John Blackburn, aged 19, a native of Dunnington . . . for coining and issuing base money"; "Martin Burrell . . . for stealing a mare", and "Frederick Gottfried and Thomas Conrat . . . for coining guineas . . . "were all executed at Tyburn on Knavesmire and buried where houses now stand on the south side of Claremont Street. In early medieval times Gillygate was within the juris-diction of St Mary's Abbey, "the abbot being lord thereof, and owner of the houses and grounds adjoining on both sides of the street"; but in 1569 a judicial enquiry ruled that it was within the jurisdiction of the Mayor and citizens.

On your right is the Salvation Army Barracks opened on Monday 26

March 1883 by 'General' William
Booth, founder of the movement.
After an open air meeting on 31
July 1881 there was a demand for
a permanent 'barracks' amongst
the Salvationist soldiers, and in
1882 "a portion of the churchyard
of St Giles" adjacent to Claremont
Terrace had been bought for £750.
The foundation stones were laid
on Monday 10 July 1882 by Alderman Agar (Lord Mayor), Miss
Emma Booth, Mrs W. Sessions, Mr
J Bass, Mr J Lumley and the Reverend A.R. Fausett . The building,
which cost about £3,000, is 70 feet
wide and 109 feet long with battlemented corner-towers of brick
and stone, with the customary colourful Army inscriptions on two
medallions at third floor level on

Snuffer in Gillygate.

the frontage as well as being inscribed on the keystone over the door.

Master builder Robert Clough (1708-91) was responsible for numbers 26
and 28 Gillygate on your left — now a medical practice — both of which
have had distinguished occupiers, including from 1823 to 1848 the Reverend John Kenrick the classical scholar and a founder of the Yorkshire
Philosophical Society. Beside the doorway of number 28 is a relic of the
aristocratic habits of former days. Inserted into the wall is a small stone
niche or tablet from which projects an inverted cone provided for the
footmen of persons of distinction to insert and extinguish their torches or
flambeaux. This was the general practice prior to the use of street lamps,
but only a few extinguishers now remain. Ladies and gentlemen returned
from their revels in the eighteenth century guided by torch-carrying 'link
boys'.

As a observer of the day poetically put it:

When in long rank a train of torches flame,
To light the midnight visits of the dame.

When King Edward IV paid a visit to the city in the fifteenth century a
hundred torches were provided by the Corporation for the firepans for
lighting the street at night during the time the King was in the city but at
other times the citizens were left to grope their own way through the dark

Protective shutters in the City walls, Marygate.

streets.

Also on the left in numbers 18 and 20 lived and died the great York artist Joseph Halfpenny (1748-1811).

Over Number 4 is the date 1891 in a terracotta scroll and number 2 has cherubs and other characters in two reliefs on the upper storey.

Turn right along Bootham to St Mary's Tower built in 1325 and at some time after the re-establishment of the King's Council in the North in 1537 the repository of all the records taken out of the religious houses north of the Trent at the time of the Dissolution of the Monasteries. At noon on 16 June 1644 a mine was exploded under it by besieging forces commanded by the Earl of Manchester. The outer half collapsed, killing some defenders and destroying most of the documents, although some were salvaged.

Immediately behind the tower lies an ancient bowling green which was probably used by those monarchs visiting York who stayed in King's Manor as well as city gentry. This is thought to be the green where highwayman John Nevison played bowls with the Lord Mayor to establish his alibi after his famous ride from London. Having robbed a traveller on the highway near London in 1673 he rode the 200 miles to York in fifteen hours at an average speed of more than twelve miles an hour, but there is little doubt that more than one horse was used

Go down Marygate and on your left you will see, in some parts of the parapets, facsimiles of the wooden shutters used in medieval times to guard the bowman against a return flight of arrows. The abbey wall, which is thirteenth and fourteenth century, is unique in that its battlements retain the grooves for these shutters, which swing on trunions. The wooden guard, after the bowman had fired his arrows in quick succession, was swung down to protect him. The grooves do not exist anywhere else on the city walls and it is doubtful if there are any others in England except possibly at Alnwick.

Marygate, looking towards the Bay Horse.

Pass Galmanhoe Lane on your right and the Coach House Hotel and Minster Inn next to which stands a building which has had a varied career. Erected early in the eighteenth century as a cotton factory it was taken over as a Union workhouse after 1764 when seventeen parishes of the city united for the purpose of Poor-law administration. It housed a hundred people and was described as "grossly unsanitary with a courtyard which was a permanent reservoir of foul air privies which were without exception in an offensive state and an open cesspool in the girl's yard." In 1850 it was taken over by the York Ragged School Committee who carried on their work here until 1858 when it was certified as an Industrial School in which capacity it continued until March 1921. The following year Manor School, York's oldest elementary school, established in 1812, was transferred here and remained until April 1942 when the buildings were damaged in the April air raid of that year. Now known as Manor Chamber it has on the wall an inscribed stone which reads:

The Manor School Founded 1812
Removed to this Site from the Kings Manor House in 1922
through the efforts of The Late Frederick James Munby.

Further down on the right is the fine seventeenth century house with carved gables called Almery Garth which recalls the fact that the adjacent land bore that name for centuries. In very early times it was the field in which the monks of St Mary's Abbey kept livestock which was charitably bestowed on them. Here too was the abbots' fish ponds, all traces of which have now vanished. John Woolman, the Quaker philanthropist, died of smallpox in this house in 1772.

Almost opposite is St Olave's Church. About 1050 Earl Siward of Northumbria built a church near his residence, which was consecrated "in the name of god and Olaf". This may have been an act of atonement for the murder of Eadulf, Earl of Bernicia, his wife's uncle, whom he had assassinated in 1041 at the instigation of King Hardicanute, receiving that earldom in addition to his own as a reward. Rebuilt in the fifteenth century, the church was badly damaged in the siege of 1644 and the roof was used as a platform for the besiegers artillery. It was repaired in 1705 with stone from St Mary's Abbey, and the present chancel was rebuilt in 1877. The pews of 1860 are of Norwegian oak and the third pew from the front on the North side boasts a leg rest for a man's wooden leg.

Drinking Fountain in Museum Street.

The six bells of this church were cast by George Dalton at his bell foundry in Stonegate in 1789 and were the last peal of bells cast for the city in the city as bell-founding died out in York shortly after they were cast. By the beginning of this century the bell frame and bell fittings were in a derelict condition and ringing had to cease. Money left by a parishioner just before the First World War to restore the tower and bells was insufficient when the work was undertaken in 1915 and, as a compromise, the bells were hung dead for chiming.

Buried in the graveyard is one of the city's most famous citizens — William Etty R.A. Born on 10 May 1787 in Feasgate, son of a miller and ginger-bread baker, he made a major contribution to the preservation of the city walls, especially Bootham Bar a model of which is held by his statue in Exhibition Square. He died in November 1849 and wanted to be buried near the Minster choir, but his tomb is here, framed by a broken arch of St Mary's Abbey.

The principal entrance in medieval times to St Mary's Abbey adjoins the church. The gate-house, which was long used as a public house bearing the sign of The Brown Cow was restored in 1840.

Go through the archway to enter Museum Gardens in which are the remains of St Mary's Abbey and on your left the Roman Multangular Tower called Elrondyng in the fourteenth century but which received its present name in 1683 when its Roman origin was recognised. It is the west angle tower of the legionary fortress and was built about AD300.

Controversy surrounded the early years of the Yorkshire Museum on your left when a highly-charged debate took place in 1844 between those who believed that God created heaven and earth in six days and those who believed that, although the Bible acknowledged God as creator, its function was not to give a detailed account of the methods of creation. Dean of York William Cockburn defended the Bible while William Buckland ably propounded the geologists view. As controversy caused by the debate simmered on for several days York Corporation decided it could not entertain both the Dean and visiting scientists. York's Lord Mayor, George Hudson, the Railway King, withdrew his formal invitation to the geologists saying "we've decided for Moses and the Dean".

Here also is the little building which cost £300 to put up 150 years ago and which was reopened in 1981 after many years of dereliction. It commemorates the inaugural meeting of the British Association for the Advancement of Science in 1831 when Dr Pearson, vice-president of the Royal Astronomical Society, promised the Yorkshire Philosophical Society two of his best instruments if they would build an observatory. True to his word he gave the society not only a four-inch telescope and a transit instrument but a sidereal clock which marks time measured by the stars, and the conical roof of his summer-house. This roof was built by John Smeaton, engineer of the Eddystone Lighthouse, and could revolve so that the telescope could be pointed anywhere in the sky.

The transit instrument enabled the society to work out the correct mean time for the city long before the Greenwich Observatory 'pips' started being broadcast throughout the country in 1924.

In 1868, Pearson's telescope was replaced by one built and installed by Thomas Cooke, one of the most eminent scientific instrument makers of his time; a York man whose firm has since become Vickers Instruments. Inside is a small museum of astronomy and wall displays outline the contributions made by two York men, the astronomer John Goodricke and instrument maker Thomas Cooke.

Of more recent vintage is the Hungarian oak planted in December 1988 to commemorate the life and work of Jim Hingston who died on 2 March 1988. He was a distinguished garden historian and wrote a history of the Yorkshire Museum for the Yorkshire Philosophical Society who founded the gardens in 1830.

Leave the gardens in Museum Street. On your left, bearing the city arms of 1880 — five lions — is an ancient drinking fountain from which water used to issue out of a lion's mouth. This was made by Job Cole, a sculptor and monumental mason who lived at 26 Lord Mayor's Walk. Turn right for the few yards back to Lendal Bridge.

Lamps on Lendal Bridge

Bibliography

George A Auden	*York 1906*	Simpkin Marshall & Co Ltd
George Benson	*York*	Blackie & Son Ltd
J Fairfax Blakeborough	*York Racecourse*	Reid Hamilton Ltd
Ivan E Broadhead	*Walkabout York*	Tetradon Publications
Ivan E Broadhead	*Portrait of the Yorkshire Ouse*	Robert Hale Ltd
J L Brockbank & W.M. Holmes	*York in English History*	A Brown & Sons
R M Butler	*The Bars and Walls of York*	Yorkshire Archaeological Society
Darrell Buttery	*The Vanished Buildings of York*	Maxiprint
Darrell Buttery	*West of York*	Countryside Publications Ltd
T P Cooper	*Down the Ouse in 1733*	Delittle Fenwick & Co
Robert Davies	*Walks Through the City of York*	Chapman & Hall Ltd
Mark Jones	*The Foss Walk*	River Foss Amenity Society
Michael Fife & Peter Walls	*The River Foss*	W Sessions Ltd
John Harvey	*York*	B. T Batsford Ltd
David Hobman	*Through Five Bridges*	David Hobman
Gordon Home	*Roman York*	Ernest Benn Ltd
John Hutchinson & D.M. Palliser	*York*	John Bartholomew & Son Ltd
Charles Knight Brunton	*This is York*	Herald Printers Ltd
Charles Knightly & Rachel Semlyen	*Lords of the City*	York City Council
Hugh N Murray	*Whittock's Bird's Eye View of City of York in 1850s*	Friends of York Art Gallery
Philip Nash	*York Quiz Book*	Philip Nash
Patrick Nuttgens	*York*	Studio Vista Ltd
Joan & Irene Pickering	*Briddon History of Fulford*	Pickering & Briddon
Ken Piggin	*Countryside Walks Around York*	Dalesman Books Ltd
Michael Pocock	*They Lived at Dringhouses*	St Edward Confessor Church
Frederick Ross	*Yorkshire Family Romance*	William Andrews & Co
W K Sessions	*Story of a Printing House*	W Sessions Ltd
John Stevens	*Knavesmire*	Pelham Books Ltd
Ronald Willis	*York As It Was*	Hendon Publishing Ltd
Ronald Willis	*Portrait of York*	Robert Hale Ltd

Index

180